SALLY B. BAER.
HGSD '78

W9-CKJ-305

THE PERSONAL GARDEN

THE PERSONAL GARDEN

Its Architecture and Design

Bernard Wolgensinger
José Daidone

VNR VAN NOSTRAND REINHOLD COMPANY

New York   Cincinnati   Toronto

Layout: Studio S + T, Lausanne
English translation: J.A. Underwood
Plans: Jean Jordano

Van Nostrand Reinhold Company Regional Offices:
New York   Cincinnati   Chicago   Millbrae   Dallas

Copyright © 1975 by Office du Livre, Fribourg (Switzerland)
Library of Congress Catalog Card Number: 74-27400
ISBN: 0-442-29569-3

All rights reserved. No part of this work covered by the copyright hereon may be reproduced or used in any form or by any means—graphic, electronic, or mechanical, including photocopying, recording, taping, or information storage and retrieval systems—without written permission of the publisher.

Printed in Switzerland

Published in 1975 by Van Nostrand Reinhold Company
A Division of Litton Educational Publishing, Inc.
450 West 33rd Street, New York, N.Y. 10001

16 15 14 13 12 11 10 9 8 7 6 5 4 3 2 1

Library of Congress Cataloging in Publication Data:

Wolgensinger, Bernard and Daidone, José
The Personal Garden,
Its Architecture and Design.

Translation of *Votre Jardin, Architecture et Art floral.*
1. Landscape gardening.
2. Landscape architecture.
I. Title.
SB473.W5813   712'.6   74-27200
ISBN 0-442-29569-3

Contents

Introduction

"A single seed holds the whole world within it"

(Buddhist proverb)

The gardens that form the subject of this book are, above all, small gardens—whether they be designed for a small patch of ground or planted in man-made receptacles—their chief characteristic being that they stand in a close relationship to the house around which or within which they are situated. This kind of integration is on the one hand made necessary by the fact that building plots are tending to get smaller and smaller and, on the other, testifies to man's increasing desire to live in closer contact with the natural environment.

Ever since man first cultivated plants in a garden—probably in Persia some 3000 years B.C.—he has been trying to recover in this way the beauties and delights of his lost paradise. Indeed the earliest gardens were a kind of magical, religious paradise, a conception that has gradually become transformed as religious preoccupations have given way to a more aesthetic, poetical approach. As the centuries and civilizations have gone by, gardens have taken on more accessible, human characteristics, until today they are designed principally for display, pleasure and relaxation.

The object of the present work is to offer the gardener the widest possible selection of typical examples of "built-in" gardens. It seeks to give some idea of the variety of national, thematic, and climatic approaches to small-garden architecture, to stimulate the imagination, spark off ideas, and open up fresh possibilities for the garden enthusiast. While pointing out a number of do's and don'ts, it presumes neither to present ready-made solutions nor to lay down rules.

Indeed it is the absence of rules that constitutes the style and wealth of the contemporary garden. Here we shall confine ourselves to pointing out the obvious natural and technical constraints and outlining the principal components that go into the creation of a beautiful garden.

Of the natural constraints undoubtedly the most limiting is climate. Wind and aridity are probably the main impinging elements against which the garden can be shielded against by means of wind-breaks, and watering. There is nothing much that can be done to control the relative humidity of the air, temperature varia-tions, nor the basic nature of the soil (for the latter, there is however the possibility of improving it by using fertilizers).

It is advisable when considering garden development to take into account the topography of the site, where the water comes in and where it drains away, the surroundings, and which views are to be preserved and which to be obscured. Nor should it be overlooked that within a particular climatic zone various microclimates can exist, the influence of which can sometimes be critical to the distribution of weather-sensitive plants. Despite consideration of climate and weather, economic factors such as cost and upkeep must constantly be borne in mind by professional and amateur alike.

A garden consists of a combination of architectural and horticultural elements. All the usual building materials are used in gardens. Stone, timber, brick, sand, concrete, glass, steel, and aluminum can all be used within the garden in accordance with the style and character of the desired whole. The same also applies to the architectural design. Pathways in particular will be governed entirely by the shape and size of the areas for which they serve. Walls, fences and steps will be made to match the house, both as concerns design and materials used, although the latter will often be more dependent on the nature of the terrain. Pergolas, pools, and fountains, being architectural set-pieces, enjoy a corresponding wealth of possibilities for style and effect.

Plants offer infinite variety, and by a careful choice, the imagination can produce delightful results. Important factors to consider when choosing plants include size when full-grown (particularly for trees and shrubs but also for flowers), shape and color according to season, ability to strike

Frugal arrangements of stones and shrubs marked by their extreme simplicity of texture form miniature landscapes in various settings on undulating land

From the mystery of dense vegetation to the austerity of dressed stone. Each element in a garden has its own composition—and its own perfect place within the whole

root, speed of growth, ecological requirements and time required for upkeep. These criteria make choice between the different classes of plant a delicate matter. Trees are particularly useful plants, so beautiful when standing alone or in groups, and can be used for their general appearance, for their color, or for casting shade. Flowering shrubs are also extremely decorative. Deciduous varieties are frequently used for hedges in conjunction with evergreen dwarf pines or firs and flowering species include everything from roses to Rhododendrons. Perennial herbs offer a very wide range of

flowers that often need little maintenance and so make suitable examples for mixed borders. Hardy annual and biennial herbs offer an even greater variety of flower forms and colors than perennials, but obviously involve greater upkeep. There is a wide selection of bulb plants from which to choose those that flower in late winter and early spring. As with perennial herbs and flowering shrubs, they serve well as easily maintained seasonal hardy flowers. Various climbers can be used to decorate pergolas or walls and floating or submerged aquatics to adorn garden pools and fountain-basins.

The garden layout, to be successful, must harmonize completely with the building with which it is associated. The ideal situation is, of course, when both the house and garden are designed together, since they can then be integrated much more easily. Sizes of structure, levels, materials, and plants will be selected and arranged in such a way as to form a coherent entity. The problem becomes more complex when a garden is being added to an existing building. Here the first requirement is to analyse the components of the existing structure; the requirements of the garden can then be defined exactly and eventually develop into a unified and harmonious whole.

The most perfect example of such integration is what we in the West regard as the "Japanese garden" since in this case the house is designed to fit the garden, the poetry of which permeates the subtly modulated architectural space in which it is set.

The gulf of history and geography between us and the Japanese garden in no way diminishes its value as a model or even as an archetype for the modern garden. The same elements of construction are used in the contemporary Western garden, al-

Each detail is richly expressive; stone, sand, moss, wood, and water can be arranged with total mastery

16

Stones emerging from a see of moss, the layout of a Kinkaku-Ji spring—two examples of how the Japanese garden gives sophisticated expression to religious symbols

though in quite different and very varied styles. Indeed this variety is what makes it so important and at the same time so difficult to take that first step in creating a garden, namely to settle on a particular theme. It is this initial definition that will set the tone of the whole garden, governing the way in which each component is treated. A garden can have a "formal" or a "natural" look, since it can share the characteristics of one or another of such widely differing historical gardens, such as the geometrical layouts of the Alhambra at Granada, and Versailles, or the natural settings of a modern botanic gar-

den. Diversity of garden structure is indicative of the spirit of our time. Gardens give aesthetic expression to man's ideas and a living example to his relationship with nature. That makes them an essential if unobtrusive ingredient of civilization itself. In perfectly expressing a man's personality, they at the same time offer a haven of security, intimacy and peace.

I. Paved and Planted Areas

Paving, the most deliberate element of a garden, is also the most relaxed and restful. Primarily functional, it enables those using the garden to indulge in a variety of activities such as playing, eating and putting their feet up without having to worry about mud and damp, while at the same time protecting the plants. It is useful for linking different parts of a garden, separating clumps of vegetation, and generally making circulation and upkeep easier.

The architectural character of paving makes it an extremely important factor in the integration of the garden and the house, both in terms of where it is laid—extending the living room floor on the same level, for example, or lining screen-walls, which often have the effect of keying the building into its plot —and in terms of its materials, which may be the same as those used to pave the inside of the house, thus creating unity and a feeling of space. The choice of layout, size, and shape of a paved area—whether a terrace or path—should take into account not only its functional and architectural relationship to the house but also its specific purpose. Children's play areas, for example, can be separated off by means of different levels and screens of ever-green shrubs. Questions of aspect and protection against prevailing winds and bad weather, or against

heat, will need to be considered in the light of local climatic conditions and the nature of the site.

The few components involved offer almost unlimited variety as regards their mode of assembly and the character of the finished product:
— Stone, for example, provides a noble material whether it is dressed or natural, in large rectangular flags, small blocks, or laid as crazy paving. Stone lends itself best to a fairly austere creation, providing a note of solemnity to the garden.
— Brick or more usually terracotta tiling can be used to create areas of warmth and color on a more intimate scale. It can be laid in any number of

1. The silhouette of a False Acacia (Robinia) sets off the softness of the light filtered through cane matting and a Vine threaded with Geraniums

ways: flat or on edge, forming crosses or squares, in herringbone, or in other patterns of varying degrees of complexity.

— Timber is occasionally used for good effect and comfort, but its advantages tend to be outbalanced by problems of maintenance (painting, impregnation, treatment against worm, etc.) and by the fact that it is comparatively fragile in certain types of humid climate. In duckboard or solid form, natural or painted, wood does have an undeniably comfortable feeling about it.

— Concrete is perhaps the most recent addition to the list of possible paving materials and already it is one of the most extensively used, being both economical and hard-wearing and having great formal possibilities. It offers a wide choice of surface textures from unrendered shuttering to various grit, pebbledash, and marble-chip renderings.

All of these materials can be used in many different ways, depending on the shape and color of the basic component and the variety of combinations it allows. A paved area derives its character from three factors: shape, color, and texture. Furthermore, whichever material is used, certain technical requirements have to be met. For example, the problem of drawing off water after rain or watering calls for planning of gradients and the placing of drains.

In nine cases out of ten, a paved area can only be considered in the context of the plants surrounding it or incorporated in it. Quite as much as by the choice and implementation of the various materials, its character will be determined by the nature of that vegetation, which may either enhance or tone down the character of the paving as such. Turf or grass planted in the joints between flags or tiles has the effect of softening their geometrical rigidity. Various constructions such as low walls and benches which contribute to the total architectural expression can in turn be qualified by evergreen shrubs or clumps of flowers in beds or pots. Particular flowers such as Aubrietia,

1

2

1. 2. A stretch of undulating lawn blends into an area of old paving lined with Fescue grasses and mosses, the whole shaded by a maple tree

Irises, Saxifrages (Saxifraga) and Ve-
ronicas, with their endless potential
for different color combinations, can
do a lot to liven up a large paved
area, whether in the form of a border
or in some geometrical arrangement
depending on the type of garden.

1   **2** **3**

1.-3. The passing year is discreetly present here in earthenware tubs in which Tulips, Geraniums and Begonias greet the changing seasons

1. A paved area at a lower level isolates the children's playground, with Geraniums, Hemp, and flowering shrubs decorating the division
2. A dense, clipped hedge of Common hornbeam contrasts with the elegance of a Japanese maple
3. A Poinsettia and Hibiscus rosasinensis, standing out sharply against white washed walls, soften the severity of the stone paving

1

2

1. A spreading Rhododendron adorns this wooden terrace
2. Sumach and persistent shrubs effect an elegant transition between their metal tub and the wood of the walls and floor
3.-7. A selection of play or relaxation areas, concealed from view by banks of dense vegetation and brightened by vivid clumps of Delphinium, Starwort, Vervain, Spiraea, and Coneflower (Rudbeckia). The paving and retaining walls are either concrete or wood

3

4

5

6

1. Square slabs of washed gravel between clumps of flowers—Leopard's bane and Forget-me-not enhance a wood-and-brick doorway
2. A paved area extending a living room
3. The rigidity of the paving is softened by the exuberance of the surrounding vegetation
4. A paved terrace forms the setting for this little pool of water-plants that a white-painted concrete back panel throws into delicate relief
5. Vine and Hibiscus rosa-sinensis stand out strongly in the Greek sun

1

3

4

5

II. Borders

Borders are a "transitional" element between the architectural and vegetative components of a garden and fulfill the function of containing and defining the flower beds while playing a secondary but still fairly important decorative role.

As a piece of architecture the border can be treated in a wide variety of ways from a formal angular pattern to a more abstract design. Often it forms the edge of a path or paved area, sharing all the same richness of color and materials. It can be built of stone, terracotta, gravel, concrete or slate, or it may be a low wall of bricks or simply a step made of stone or brick or large logs of wood.

The plants of a border should be

visualized with the architecture in mind. Geometric shapes can be achieved by using such shrubs as Dwarf Box (Buxus sempervirens) or Santolina that can be trimmed, or perennial herbs such as Feathered pinks (Dianthus) and Dwarf Iris, or a much less organized arrangement by using low-growing spreading perennials or annuals.

Problems of maintenance will influence its composition, as will the periods during which the garden is in use. Borders can be in full flower for a season and afterwards remain in foliage. They can remain in flower all the time, or they can be made up largely of evergreen plants—bamboos (Sinoarundinaria), Cotoneas-ters, dwarf conifers, mosses and ornamental grasses—but still with clumps of flowers here and there to reflect the seasons such as Irises, Forget-me-nots (Myosotis) and Polyanthus (Primula polyantha) in the spring; Arum lilies, Dahlias, Freesias, and Chrysanthemums in the autumn. Borders also vary according to country, climate, and the nature of the soil. The typical cactus border of the Mediterranean region for example is very different from the bushy borders characteristic of northern countries. Sculpture too has its part to play: structures in stone, iron, or wood or simply sea-bleached tree-roots can sometimes lend considerable dignity to this transitional but none the less important element of the garden.

1

1. Here the formality of concrete flags is modified by the roundness of loose cobbles and by the sharpness of a Firethorn. Plantain lilies enhance the lawn

1. The austerity of this steel sculpture fits in well with the dwarf conifers. The concrete flags with their washed-gravel facing are softened by spreading plants
2. Bamboos form a luxuriant background for the dwarf conifers and Azalea in the foreground

1. A clump of ornamental grass set off by pebbles and brick paving
2. Shiny ornamental grasses lighten the severity of the architecture
3. A natural, spontaneous-looking composition provides a visual link between the garden and the adjoining vegetation

1

2

3

4. Considerable decorative effect is achieved by edging washed-gravel paving with large cobbles
5. One or two potted cacti are the only plants in this inorganic border
6. Austerity and strength characterize this composition of cobbles, grass, and prefabricated concrete flags

4

5

6

1. A dwarf pine, a Cotoneaster, and a tuft of Fescue grass frame a composition of Rudbeckia spinosa and Hibiscus rosa-sinensis
2. The edge of the paving is hidden beneath a delicate fringe of Plantain lilies
3. Fescues and bamboos enlighten a stone border

4

4. Combining the functions of border and retaining-wall, these logs mediate effectively between the soft-textured lawn and the hard pebbles below

1. Grass and pebbles are here separated by a simple line of bricks
2. A dense clump of wiry grasses provides a counterpoint to this stone border
3. Given its shape and texture, this tree root stands out against its background of dense vegetation

1

2

3

III. Flower Beds

Banks of flowers or ornamental shrubs, broad expanses of vegetation, and mixed borders are here grouped under the general heading of "flower beds". The flower bed is either surrounded by a lawn or paths or backs onto the house or an enclosure of some kind. It is a common feature in gardens of temperate countries where it is easy to grow annuals and perennials together in profusion. It is an essentially horticultural element, but where it complements or accompanies an architectural feature such as the house, a pergola, a wall or an enclosure of some kind, it constitutes an effective link between the garden and the architecture since it is so adaptable. Its design should match the spirit of the overall composition.

The character of a flower bed will depend to a great extent on the material with which the surrounding paths or walls are made i.e. whether wood, sand, grass, or stone. In northern temperate countries, flower beds usually last only for a part of the year and for the rest of the time remain quite unobtrusive. This means that their position must be chosen carefully in accordance with the garden's principal theme. Other factors which must be taken into account are exposure to sunlight, rainfall and the nature of the soil, for it is impossible to make a lot of different species with quite different ecological requirements grow in the same place. The maintenance involved is usually quite considerable, especially if the flower bed is to remain in bloom for as long as possible.

Evergreen decorative shrubs (bamboos, dwarf conifers) make a solid basis to which one can add a whole range of annuals and perennials. A harmonious arrangement of these plants will be governed by color, by their growth pattern, by their flowering period, and of course by shape and height. Juggling with these factors to create perspective effects through form and color is a difficult art, particularly in the case of highly complex mixed borders. Depending on the season one chooses to feature, one can use bulbs and spreading perennials for the spring; particularly annuals and herbaceous or woody perennials—such as Wallflower (Antirrhinum), Cosmos, Marigold (Tagetes), Gaillardia and Larkspur (Delphinium)—for summer; and for autumn, Chrysanthemum, Starwort (Aster), Tickseed, Coreopsis, and Coneflower (Rudbeckia). Possible background plants are Hollyhocks (Althaea rosea), climbers such as Bignonia, Virgin's bower (Clematis) and Jasmin (Jasminum), or a hedge of evergreen shrubs such as Box or conifers.

This wide variety of plants from which to choose make flower beds the gayest, most exuberant, and most colorful part in the garden.

1

1. Framed by brick and wood, a spontaneous composition of Delphinium, Columbine, Iris, and bamboo enlivens the geometric formality of the architecture

1. Concrete flags faced with washed gravel frame these rectangles planted on the model of the Moroccan *ryad*
2. Against the background of a pergola and the stone wall of the house a Yew stands in a setting of Hollyhock, Delphinium, Candytuft, Gypsophila elegans, and Campanula carpatica
3. Pinks, Delphinium, and a Rambler rose mingle with the backdrop of trees and evergreen shrubs

1 2

1. Here the severity of a brick path is tempered by a selection of roses
2. Honeysuckle, an ornamental grass and dwarf pine interspersed with annuals enliven this garden wall
3. Cotoneaster, Barberry, Scabious, Helianthemum, Marguerite, Lavender and Candytuft follow a selection of bulbs—Narcissus, Tulip, Crocus, Hyacinth and Snowdrop—against the background of a hedge of evergreen trees including a Blue Atlas cedar

1

2 3

1

2

1. With the house at the rear and the entrance steps to one
   side, a composition of evergreen shrubs—Cotoneaster, and
   an ornamental grass (Pennisetum)—enlivens bright clumps
   of Phlox and Coneflower (Rudbeckia)
2. A classic mixed border, its rich coloring set off by an austere
   background of conifers

IV. Walls, Fences and Hedges

The chief functions of enclosures are for keeping off prevailing winds, marking the boundary of a property, and providing protection and privacy. All these requirements can be fulfilled in a pleasant and decorative fashion. Conceived in the spirit of the garden as a whole, enclosures may occasionally take up all of the garden. They may be constructed of building materials, they may consist entirely of vegetation, or they may be a mixture of both. Whilst fulfilling their primary function, whatever that may be, enclosures can also be used for more subtle or aesthetic architectural purposes, for example to draw attention to a garden feature, or to narrow down a field of view. They will be designed in accordance with the architecture, materials, and style of the house, and their size and situation in the surrounding landscape make them extremely important integrating factors.

A wall or fence is first and foremost a piece of building, subject to certain laws and constraints. Any material can be used in the manufacture of the enclosure ranging from stone to concrete aggregate by way of brick, glass, and aluminum. The material chosen will of course govern the nature of the construction, since each substance has its own special requirements. The foundations will be dictated by the nature of the terrain, the drainage problem, and the degree of wind-resistance of the enclosure to be built, i.e. whether it is to be solid or perforated. Consequently one's choice of material will be to some extent determined by the site.

A hedge or planted enclosure will be governed, as regards choice of plants, by its principal function and by the desired end result. Good protection is best provided by a mixture of thorn bushes and evergreen shrubs such as Hawthorn (Crataegus), Barberry (Berberis), Firethorn (Pyracantha), Olive (Olea europea), Spindle-tree (Euonymus europaeus), Lavender (Lavandula), Rosemary (Rosmarinus officinalis), cactus, Jujube (Zizyphus jujuba). Hed-

1. A stone enclosing wall covered with Virgin's bower is here echoed by low-retaining walls planted with Tulips and Aubrietia

ges for clipping can, in temperate climates, be planted with White cedar (Thuja occidentalis) or Box, well-known for its use in French formal gardens. Flowering hedges could incorporate Forsythia, Hawthorn, Colliers Broom (Cytisus scoparius), Rush broom (Viminaria), etc., while Lavender and Rosemary will make even the most forbidding-looking hedge smell quite sweet. A number of conifers such as juniper (Juniperus), Cypress (Cupressus) and Spruce (Picea) lend themselves to a much nobler type of hedge. Occasionally stringent ecological conditions may determine the choice of certain types of hedge plant; at the seaside, for example, hardy plants such as the Spindle-tree, Hydrangea, or Tamarisk (Tamarix) will be required.

Hedges and other built enclosures are sometimes developed together in order to complement one another: the rectangular character of a fence or wall, for example, lends structure to a somewhat free-growing hedge. On the other hand a creeper, such as a Virgin's bower or a Wisteria, will soften the rigidity of a brick or concrete wall.

Similarly, dwarf rockery plants may decorate the chinks of a stone wall. In fact any kind of combination is permissible, depending really only on the climate and the basic compositional choice between harmony or contrast. Apart from these simple

1. A simple wooden fence completely covered with roses and evergreen shrubs forms a spreading enclosure that merges with the Foxgloves behind and the Virgin's bower on the porch roof
2. Virgin's bower, Lily and rose disguise the harshness of this high cast-concrete wall

1

2

suggestions there are many variants in design. A flower bed can easily be developed as a hedge. Similarly a mixed border can be expanded into a seasonal hedge and as such enjoy a range of different possibilities.

The gate is an essential part of the enclosure and one that shares the same characteristics as regards materials and treatment. It also constitutes a visitor's first encounter with the house, and this presentational, ambassadorial function consequently bestows on it great importance. It contains in embryo the style and architectural options of the house and of its relationship with the surrounding garden. Functional and technical constraints assume more importance in the gate than in the rest of the enclosure. It must be solid, it must be effective, and it must be easy to open and shut. And remember in this respect that it caters equally for the pedestrian and the motorized vehicle. It must provide easy and rapid access for those on foot, and this should if possible be independent of the vehicle access; a gate wide enough to admit cars will be heavy and awkward for pedestrians to use.

A final consideration that must be borne in mind when designing the enclosure is the fact that a hedge or wall provides a very effective windbreak, or may, depending on its size and position, create a local microclimate that will influence the plants growing in its vicinity. Shade alone can have the effect of discouraging vigorous growth of certain sun-loving plants whilst, on the other hand, providing ideal conditions for shade plants such as ferns. These problems can be solved with patience and by careful observation of developments within the affected areas. Taken together with the whole problem of integration, however, they do show that the design and composition of an enclosure—such simple matters at first sight—involve a degree of complexity and ambiguity that is commensurate with the importance of this vital ingredient of every successful garden.

1. The design of this fence echoes and blends with that of the pool. Rose, Lavender, Delphinium, and bamboo provide an exquisite setting

54

1. A Rhododendron shrouds the foot of a Judas tree against a fence with a marked vertical pattern
2. A Wisteria casts its intricate shadow on a glass partition
3. Tulip tree, Sumach and Acanthus dance arabesques before a hedge of Cherry laurel

1   2   3

V. Ponds and Fountains

A pond or a fountain, no matter how small, lends an extraordinary degree of life and poetry to a garden. The presence of water will pleasantly cool the air in a hot climate, brighten the atmosphere and make a restricted, busy space look larger and more relaxed. A pond may be artificial or natural, it may be the dominant element in a garden, setting the tone, or it may be no more than a small detail, fitting into the whole concept. This process is greater facilitated when it is built by hand and can be related architecturally to the house. It may of course be developed inside the house, or between the house and garden linking interior with the exterior. The swimming pool is simply a more utilitarian and antiseptic version of the ornamental bathing lake. It will dictate the character of a garden, which will tend in any development to be defined in relation to the pool. The artificial pond is the general solution for a small garden and this calls for a certain density of composition. Stone is the usual material for the lip, but brick, mosaic, and concrete are also common. A fountain will often take the form of a piece of sculpture. There is even room for art in the plumbing as well. The inlet piping, for example, can take a variety of symbolic forms such as dolphins, cornucopias or cherubs or, in a more abstract vein, it can exploit all the possibilities of metal sculpture. Stagnant water is always to be avoided, and it will be necessary to add fresh water periodically to a pond or to provide a permanent water feed, however slow this might be. This will undoubtedly involve having an overflow pipe, and there must also be some means of completely draining the pond at intervals. On a sloping site and with sufficient water one can engineer a tinkling stream or a sparkling waterfall that will make a spectacular contribution to any style of garden.

The plants used to decorate ponds and fountain-basins are of two types—those that grow in the water and those that grow around it. In the water one finds various species with floating leaves planted in submerged tubs or plots of earth that must be carefully contained for ease of upkeep. Water-lilies (Nymphaea) are the most common, but one can also use Water-Plantain (Alisma plantago-aquatica), which is flowery but rampant, or the Cape pond-weed (Aponogeton distachyus). In the soil around the pond or fountain, all varieties of flowers and shrubs are possible. Main criteria for selection include shape, as enhanced by their reflection in the water, color, so as to harmonize with the water, or decorative effect in relation to the surrounding wall or paving.

Typically aquatic plants are found in and around natural ponds, the banks of which may be adorned with marsh plants or simply plants that like damp soil. Attractive examples include Papyrus (Cyperus papyrus), Japanese Iris (Iris laevigata), Bulrush (Typha angustifolia), Marsh Marigold (Caltha palustris), Loosestrife (Lysimachia), Bog Bean (Menyanthes trifoliata) and Astilbe cattleya.

1. An example of an artificial pond. The concrete and gravel surround is relieved by various Fescues against a background of bamboo
2. A large lawn with its skirt of perennials provides the perfect setting for this fountain-sculpture
3. Water-lilies and reeds counter the stiffness of this rectangular composition

1

2 3

1. Almost an extension of the living room, this pond of rectangular design lends unity to the scene. Rowan tree and rush, together with their reflections, fill out this composition

2. An oasis of Japanese-style coolness amid dense vegetation

3. An unusual example of a swimming pool treated as an ornamental pond, at one with the surrounding vegetation

1 **2** **3**

4

4. An atmosphere of romantic harmony reigns over this simple pond—shaded by Sumach and Cotoneaster—the Ivy-clad wall, and the squares as paving

1. A strict, modular pattern of square concrete flagstones is relieved here by its vigorous outline and by a tangle of Iris and rushes
2. A composition in water and dressed and natural stone. In the background, Sennapod and Potentilla
3. Dwarf Mountain pine and Spiraea lining a calmly geometric pond
4. Nature in the wild—but wholly man-made
5. A bird-bath framed by perennials

1

2 3 4 5

1. A balanced composition of cylindrical barrels of various sizes, planted with Water-lily, Rush, and Dwarf Bulrush

2.-4. A sharply defined pond forms the center of this balanced garden. The plants are mostly perennials, set in a vigorous pattern of concrete flags faced with washed gravel. Water-lilies and other aquatics lend an exotic note

1

2

3   4

1. Here a variety of mineral and plant textures are linked by a strong design
2. The pure lines of this metal basin stand out against the tangle of vegetation
3. The strange, poetic harmony of water and lush vegetation

2

3

1

2

3

1.-3. Here water is treated as a reflecting medium in the context of a strictly geometrical architectural composition

VI. Pergolas

Pergolas are open post-and-beam structures designed to support climbing plants or to provide shade and seclusion. They fall into two main categories: those that form an integral part of a house, extending it or forming an enclave within it, whether at ground level or on a terrace, and those that are free-standing, independent of the house. Pergolas invite architectural expertise and horticultural imagination in the creation of an interesting walkway and a backdrop of a particular prospect. They can be built of brick, wood, or metal and they can be rectangular or arched in shape. A pergola will usually be paved to match the house with clay tiles or stone flags, or to

1. A natural brick floor and painted brick walls point up the simplicity of this pergola of painted wood adorned with a vine
2. This vine-covered pergola forms an integral part of the house
3. Cane matting has the effect of softening the light
4. Bougainvillaea and Geranium mingle with a vine to form a bright, gay wall of vegetation

1

2 3

4

match the garden with grass or gravel in order to provide a link between the two. Each material can be treated in a variety of ways, depending on the style selected. Uncut timber with the bark intact will give a rustic character; square, rectangular, or round painted posts and beams lend themselves to a more architectural effect. Beams can be widely spaced or they can be placed close together so as to give shade or to support a cover of cane matting. Metal needs less support and can be made to look more elegant. It is sometimes used for the uprights, supporting wooden beams, or it may take the form of a skeleton on which wires are strung to take the plants.

Brick or stone masonry, which gives a more massive look, is primarily used for the construction of pillars, although it may also be used to form flying buttresses or to provide cool arches and vaults in hot countries. There are various kinds of climbing plant to cover this architectural structure. Wisteria, different types of Vine (Vitis), Climbing Persicary (Polygonum), Jasmin, Honeysuckle (Lonicera), Rambler rose (Rosa wichuriana), and Virgin's bower will twist around each post and beam, while annual flowers, spreading plants and ornamental grasses hug the foot of each upright. The vegetation will dictate the character of the structure. A delicate skeleton will call for the elegance of Virgin's bower or Passion-flower (Passiflora caerulea), the color of Bougainvillaea will enliven the white brick pillars of a typical Mediterranean pergola. Works of art will find a natural place here, marking the rhythm of the bays or when set in the longitudinal axis, stressing their symmetry. Finally in pergolas the best protection against the sun is that provided by dense climbers such as Vine and Bignonia, which filter the light in a friendly, welcoming way.

1. An all-wood structure of posts, planks, beams, and boards with plants providing a quiet accompaniment

2

1. Notice the subtle harmony between stone, pines, and the sturdy timber skeleton of the pergola
2. Vine, bamboo and Sumach match the delicacy of the cane matting
3. Here is a pergola made of uncut timber, to give it a rustic character. Bulb plants and perennials ring the foot of each upright

1

1. The wooden uprights of this pergola find vertical echoes in Yew, Hollyhock and Delphinium
2. A shady pergola rounds off the expanse of lawn and stone paving

VII. Patios

The patio originally conceived as an inner open-air courtyard of Spanish houses is now used in many dwellings in hot countries to keep them cool by transpiration and shade of the plants. It provides a most perfect example of the integrated garden, since it is defined purely in relation to its architectural context. Either the house opens onto it through only one or two doorways, as in the case of the Spanish or Moroccan patios with their central pool and a small number of carefully chosen plants, or the house may open directly into the patio often in the center of the house, with this becoming a room in its own right. In temperate countries the patio provides an ideal hot-house or conservatory atmosphere all the year round, giving plenty of opportunity for the cultivation of exotic plants.

The functions of a patio are quite variable. It can provide circulation between the living room and the bedrooms or between the dining room and kitchen or living room; it can also serve as the dining room itself, or it can exist simply as a decorative feature.

The flooring of the patio will depend on its function. If the patio is to be incorporated into the general use of the house (as a passageway or as a room in its own right), it will be best to pave or tile it. Any material can be used, but tougher materials such as stone or terracotta are preferable because they stand up to water and damp. A further consideration is that the floor should be given a slight gradient to draw off excess water, whether it comes from the sky or the watering can. The natural place for the pool or fountain will be at the lowest point, i.e. where the water collects. The fountain may be placed against one wall, to which it will give a decorative effect.

Where the patio does not serve the purposes of circulation or where its function is purely ornamental, the floor can be turfed or planted with pearl grass and dotted with stepping stones.

The walls may be of stone, rendered

1. The strictly rectangular composition of this patio is enlivened by the abundance of the vegetation; note particularly the vine, the Buddleja, the Cypress and the Phoenix palm

1. Bamboos, Camellias, and conifers form islands in a sea of gravel
2. A maple and Rhododendrons adorn this bathroom garden
3. A dry garden with one or two conifers

with concrete or plaster, of painted brickwork or of glass in a wooden or metal frame and should share the diversity of the architecture. In the case of a covered patio the architectural element will obviously dominate. The roof may be of the conventional type, lit by a number of skylights; it could also consist of a flat or pyramidal glazed structure in a metal framework or it may be a sloping wooden structure with sheets of plexiglass at various intervals. Good ventilation is essential in order to avoid condensation on the glazed surfaces, and some sort of heating system must be provided to give the plants optimal growing conditions throughout the winter. In most cases a comparatively low-powered system ensuring a right temperature of around 7 degrees C will be adequate.

An open-air patio will need most protection against the sun. Perhaps the best way of obtaining a pleasantly filtered light is by using plants. Something similar to cane matting stretched over wires offers an economical solution, although various climbers such as the Grape-vine (Vitis vinifera) or Kangaroo-vine (Cissus antarctica), Bignonia or Passion-flower will add a more poetic note. At night a patio lends itself to a wide variety of lighting effects ranging from a mellow effect to a slightly mysterious or even to a distinctly eerie one. Indirect lighting at floor-level, spotlights aimed at certain plants, standard lamps or ornamental lanterns fixed to the wall to spread a diffused and restful light are some of the most widely adopted solutions. The choice will depend entirely on the lighting concept of the house as a whole. Another possibility is to leave the patio in romantic semi-darkness, lit only by the rooms round it. The horticultural aspect of a patio will throw into relief the principal features of its architectural conception. If the idea is to stress the purity and proportions of the architecture, a few plants will be enough: for example, the classic pattern of four cypresses, planted in a square around a small pool or a few pot plants arranged simply around the lip of a small fountain. Low borders of Myrtle (Myrtus) or a clipped Box are often used. Dramatic effects can be obtained with few or no flowers, with the possible exception of a climbing plant or two such as a Wisteria, a Passion-flower or a trailing species of Climbing Persicary. Where, however, the plant arrangement takes precedence over the architecture of the patio, one has a whole range of climbers from which to choose (Asparagus, Bougainvillaea, Passion-flower) in conjuction with various spreading plants such as a St John's wort (Hypericum calycinum), Periwinkles (Vinca), Co-reopsis, Day-lily (Hemerocallis), and above all the many varieties of Meditteranean and semi-tropical plants—Garden fig (Ficus lyrata), palms, cacti, and so on. In the favorable conditions provided by a patio, garden plants usually grow exceptionally well and the coexistence problem will rapidly become acute, since some plants, particularly the climbers, can literally exclude the others. One must either achieve a careful balance at the initial planting stages or keep a close eye on later developments and indulge in a bit of judicious pruning now and then. Despite the minor constraints a patio of any character, however large or small, is a very concentrated garden, allowing the very greatest possible freedom. It is both a spectacle and a living space, functional and magical in one.

1. Around the shady Chestnut in the center of the patio a feeling of perspective is created by the creeper-clad walls extending into the house

2. An architect-designed plant tub, matching the flooring and containing miniature landscape

1. 2. These bamboos enliven the first-floor living room with their trunks and the terrace above with their foliage
3.-5. Japanese architecture blends the modern with the tradional; contemporary garden architecture pays homage to tradition, in both atmosphere and visual representation

1

2

3

4

5

1. A traditional garden links the modern wing of this house with the old part
2. 3. A flowering Pear, a Laburnum, tubs and troughs of flowers, and some concrete furniture are the only decorations in this brick and slate patio overlooked from the living room through full-length windows
4. The reconstituted primeval forest

1

2

3

4

1. As well as linking all of the rooms together, this patio is the visual center of the house with its tropical plants of Bougainvillaea, Passion-flower, Jasmin and Allamanda carthartica. The top lighting gives the effect of an insulated environment
2. Looking through into the library
3. The view from the living room
4. Looking across from the library towards the kitchen

1

2
3
4

1.-3. This Mexican grotto patio planted with a Dragon tree, a fern and a Philodendron conjures up something of the atmosphere of the primeval forest

1

2

3

VIII. Indoor Plants

Reduced to its simplest expression, a garden can consist of a single plant. The city-dwelling man, totally deprived of natural surroundings, sometimes feels the need to create a little corner of greenery for himself, even if it is so domesticated as to border on the symbolic. In doing so he decorates his house or flat with flowers and pot plants. The pots come in various sizes and shapes, such as cylinders, cones, and cubes and in a variety of colors and materials, which are either porous (red earthenware), or non-porous (china, metal, or glazed earthenware). The pots can be arranged in gravel beds in large zinc troughs, lined up on a shelf, grouped on a table, or simply

1

1. A Hydrangea does something to tame the aggressiveness of this Spurge, which the top lighting dramatizes
2. Large windows create a greenhouse climate that fosters the Papyrus, Rubber plant, and dwarf palm growing in this indoor trough
3. A sober collection of potted plants

2

3

suspended individually in a variety of places. If the house is built on one floor it is possible to accommodate a deep trough of proper soil in which larger plants—Garden fig, Philodendron, or a palm (Dracaena or Phoenix), for example—can grow and flourish. Great care must be taken over the positioning of such a trough, however, because most plants are attracted by light and will turn their leaves towards the source of it. It must be remembered that it is light, too, that makes them flower and maintain their pigmentation. On the other hand, light can inhibit growth and, sometimes even, full sunlight in a temperate climate is to be avoided. Also remember that artificial light can in some measure make up for the absence of natural light but can never wholly replace it.

Most indoor plants are exotic in origin. Indeed it is only indoors that their natural climate can to some extent be reconstituted. Even so one important element that is difficult to control satisfactorily is the relative humidity of the air. Certain plants, such as Copperleaf (Acalypha) and Caladium, like a warm, humid atmosphere; others, such as Ivy (Hedera helix), Aucuba, Aspidistra, and Philodendron scandens, are hardier. Others again need special care such as African violets (Saintpaulia ionantha), Tillandsia, and Bird's nest fern (Asplenium nidus-avis). Some plants dislike heat and need to be placed in a cool place for the night (Cyclamen, Azalea, Cineraria, Hyacinth (Hyacinthus); others, such as most cacti, can withstand dryness.

But in spite of the fact that each plant has its own requirements it is a simple matter, given a selection of hardy species and the right kind of upkeep, to embellish the most restricted space with a little bit of nature, providing everyone with a corner, be it sober or luxuriant, in which he can relax and perhaps lose himself in reverie.

1. Top lighting in a corridor fosters the growth of this Garden fig

1

1. An onion and a selection of leaf cacti in pots
   arranged simply on a shelf and on the floor
   create an exotic garden that provides a visual
   link with the curtain of trees beyond the terrace

IX. Steps

Gardens with a gradient in excess of ten per cent will need to have steps connecting the various different levels. The extent of the gradient difference will determine how important a part those steps will play in the overall arrangement of the garden. If the entire garden is very steep, it may become a single flight of steps, or rather a series of terraces, each of which can be treated separately. At the other extreme, if the garden is only partly steep, then only a few steps are involved and they will simply become another element in the general composition though an architecturally important one, because a flight of steps can be a crucial integrating factor not only in terms of its shape but also in terms of the chosen materials. Steps will expand the other built elements of the garden—walls, fences, ponds and paving—thus giving a sense of unity. Whether it is built in a straight line, a curving arc, in a steep flight or laid out as gradines (very low, very wide steps), a flight of steps can have the effect of either attenuating or accentuating differences of level. A handrail along the side of a flight of steps will be a further important linking element between the architecture and the vegetation depending on both the form it takes and the material chosen for construction. The materials will generally be the same as those used for masonry:

natural or dressed stone, bricks and concrete, the latter being used in any case for the foundations and such retaining walls as may be necessary to key the structure to the site. Depending on the desired effect, each material will be used in conjunction with the forms suited to it: straight steps of dressed and polished stone will lend a certain nobility to a symmetrical composition; a relaxed, rustic arrangement will call for a winding stairway of crazy paving with grass and flowers planted in the joints. Brick is a much warmer material highly suited to small flights of a few steps buttressing or simply edging a brick-paved or sanded terrace. A rockery laid out with a series

1. 2. Here the whole garden is a stairway, with an intermediate terrace covered with Morning glory and a little lawn in the shade of a Fig tree

1

2

1. At the top of the steps is a tiny pond decorated with Delphinium, Iris, and Campanula
2. Cotoneaster and Japanese maple form the background to this rich mixture of textures: timber, brick, and washed-gravel flagstones
3. Coneflower (Rudbeckia), rose, and Lavender provide a gay accompaniment to this short flight of steps
4. Juniper, Sumach, and other evergreen plants stress and yet somehow relieve the severity of this flight of stone steps

of flat stones for one to stand easily on can make a most attractive landscaped stairway.

Timber, too, is a material that is frequently used, and in a variety of ways: in its raw, uncut form it provides a kind of prefabricated element for nosings, risers, or treads; in the form of logs placed side by side and not too high, it offers a useful solution for one or two very long steps, retaining and moulding the terrain. It can also, of course, be used as planed planks and boards to build a more elaborate type of stairway, as, for example in conjunction with a duckboard terrace such as is often found in seaside houses.

Concrete, together with its various facing mediums (gravel, marble, etc.), makes up for an unexciting appearance by its superior technical potential, particularly when used in a overhanging section. Steps that seem to spring from a wall or float up a bank or slope give a tremendous impression of lightness and elegance.

Whichever material is eventually selected, the stairway can be decorated or disguised and virtually concealed by the plants growing over it, around or on the steps. Again it is the style and character of the whole garden that will dictate one's choice of plants, for no species is specific to a stairway. Clipped or naturally grown shrubs and trees—e.g. Horn-

1   2   3   4

beam (Carpinus betulus) and Box—can give a certain rhythm to a straight, symmetrical flight of steps. A friendlier, less symmetrical arrangement can be to use shrubs on one side of the stairway and to plant the other side with clumps of ferns, roses (Rosa), Juniper, Sumach (Rhus), Fescue (Festuca), and other low-growing or spreading plants. A bank covered with Ivy and overgrowing the steps that surmount it makes a romantic composition. An interesting arrangement of steps is one lined with grass and decorated with rock plants such as Saxifrages, Aubrietias, Alyssums, Campanulas, Pearlworts (Sagina), Pinks and Helianthemums. When planted at the margins of the steps and possibly on the retaining walls as well, where few people tread, such plants will serve to integrate the stairway with the rest of the garden. The interface needing the greatest attention of all is the transition between the manufactured step and the bare soil. Here no one walks and there is nothing to prevent one from planting annuals and perennials galore.

A flight of steps can be successfully combined with other garden elements—with rockeries and walls, for example—which will extend it naturally at the sides, or with a pergola, which may endorse it in a decorative tunnel overgrown with climbers. It may even, on the model of the famous Generalife gardens at Granada, take the form of a fountain and, planted accordingly, become a very special place, a sanctuary of coolness and beauty.

1

1. Rose, fern, and Lily-of-the-valley tone down
the rustic stonework

1. A stairway-garden laid out in gradines, with the vegetation enhancing the architecture. The treads give way to flowers, which in turn give way to ever-green shrubs
2. A flight of overhanging steps, two of which are extended to form retaining shelves or borders. Fescues discreetly point up the different levels
3. An original and dynamic blend of grass and paving

1

2

3

1. Encroached upon by Ivy, shrubs and crowned
   with Lavender, this flight of steps fits in well
   with the different levels of house and retaining
   wall

X. Rockeries

Originally, the rockery or "Alpine garden", as it is called, was an attempt to reproduce the mountain environment and its flora on a smaller scale. The original alpine gardens developed in the gardens of alpine village houses—in Switzerland, in Austria, and in southeastern France. Subsequently all sorts of spreading plants of similar habit to alpines have been added to the alpine garden, perennial plants growing close to the ground, often with large flowers with an ability to colonize large areas and needing very little soil. All that is left of the natural alpine gardens today is a more or less pronounced irregularity of level, whether naturally or artificially obtained, and a generally rocky appearance.

A rockery lends itself marvellously to the integration of house and garden, being easily adaptable to any architectural style through the medium of the choice and arrangement of the stones and plants that make it up. Areas that can be treated in this way are natural banks, for example, or banks created in the course of building the house such as a garage access or terrace foundations. A rockery is generally fairly small and requires constant upkeep although this need by no means be strenuous. The stones to make up the rockery will be chosen according to various criteria: the nature and color of the plants to go between them, and the general desired effect whether friendly and delicate or rustic and perhaps a natural appearance. They will be rough-textured or smooth, in rounded columns or divided into bifid spirals. They will be positioned in such a way so as to retain little pockets of earth in which various dwarf plants can grow. When chalks and limestones are chosen, one must choose plants carefully and grow those that are adapted to calcicole conditions. Granite, shale, and millstone grit are all useful materials for making rockeries without creating stringent ecological conditions. The formality of the arrangement will be dictated by the desired effect wheth-

1. Against a background of Honeysuckle and Rhododendron, here is a lively rockery planted with Iris, Delphinium, Broom, Yucca, Lavender and a Dwarf spruce

er irregular or symmetrical, using stones of more or less the same or very different sizes. A stepped arrangement with ever-increasing strips of soil towards the top of the rockery will provide for an increased density of vegetation towards the apex to create a perspective effect that will make the rockery look larger than it is. In fact the question of perspective needs to be studied very carefully from every angle because this is one of the successful rockery designer's trump cards. Different perspective effects together with the selection and arrangement of stones and plants are the ingredients with which he conjures up a miniature natural landscape or, if more imaginative, a world of poetic fantasy. For example, on the analogy of the Japanese garden, carefully designed areas of gravel or sand can represent a sea, a river, or simply a place easy on the eye.

It is absolutely essential to choose and.arrange one's stones in relation to the plants that are to be cultivated. One's choice of plants, too, will be dictated by the kind of rockery desired. They can be selected in terms of groups or in terms of individual color and shape. Both perennials and annuals can be used. The season and duration of flowering as well as the look of the plant in its vegetative state must all be taken into consideration. Robust or re-

1.-4. Four examples of the traditional rockery. Arabis, Alyssum, Forget-me-not, Candytuft, Saxifrage, Rhododendrons, and conifers are arranged with a certain naturalness

2

1

3

4

fined, brightly or neutrally colored, quiet or jazzy—whatever the character of a rockery, it is always possible to find a desired combination of plants. There are autumn rockeries and spring rockeries, rockeries that are permanently in flower and others designed to develop from a state of luxuriant exuberance to one of stark simplicity.

Perennials are widely used for the obvious fact that they last longer and also because they require less attention. Shrubs such as Azalea, Rhododendron, Barberry, Heather (Erica), Cotoneaster, and Mahonia can grow to a fair size and will be planted with this in mind.

Aromatic herbaceous perennials such as Alyssum, Milfoil (Achillea), Columbine (Aquilegia), Arabis, Campanula, Starwort, Pinks, Gentian (Gentiana), Gypsophila, Lavender, Polyanthus, Phlox, Sage (Salvia), Saxifrages (Saxifraga), Thyme (Thymus) and other scented plants can be mixed with bulb plants: Colchicum and Tulip (Tulipa), etc. Color harmony is particularly important and at the same time very difficult, because the range is so enormous. This limitless variety shows what a wealth of possibilities a rockery offers, allowing almost uninhibited imagination and sensitive expression. Seen in this light, a rockery may represent the most faithful reflection of the gardener's personality.

1

1. A rock garden that matches the strength of the architecture. The slender, airy elegant bamboos in the foreground have the effect of humanizing the whole garden

1

1. The rockery at its simplest—pebbles of all sizes
   piled at the foot of a retaining wall of logs

XI. The Balcony-Garden

Depending on its size and aspect, every balcony is capable of accommodating a small garden. The architectural element will obviously dominate here in the form of a balustrade, which might be either solid concrete, wood, plexiglass or an open steel or aluminum railing; the balcony-garden will be designed with this in mind. It will either take advantage of the architecture including additional tubs and troughs in terms of form and color or it will be concealed behind a bank of vegetation.

If the balcony is already fitted with a built-in plant trough, one has only to fill it with the desired flowers and possibly add a few more standing or suspended tubs or pots. If no built-in provision for cultivation has been made, remember that a balcony-garden is most effective when created in the spirit of the existing architecture. It is important nevertheless to check first of all whether the balcony is strong enough to support several tubs of plants: pot plants can weight a considerable amount.

Climbers are perhaps the most spectacular plants to cultivate on a balcony. Whether in a dense mass or as single plants, their stems and foliage will add a note of freedom and imagination to the fairly formal lines of most balconies. They also provide effective protection against the sun, softening and tinting the light that filters through them.

Climbing Persicaries, Wisterias, Honeysuckles, Virgin's bowers, and Rambler roses will all eventually acclimatize to a balcony if planted in pots big enough to give them a sufficient quantity of nutrients. Most plants need relatively little earth to make good balcony growers. All kinds of low-growing and spreading plants, e.g. bulb plants—Crocus, Daffodil (Narcissus), Colchicum, Tulip—brighten up the spring and autumn, various Fescue grasses and evergreen shrubs such as Myrtle and Box provide pleasant greenery all year round, and a selection of annuals and perennials—Forget-me-not, Lily (Lilium), Violet (Viola), Polyanthus, Campanula, Pink and Petunia—to add vivid dashes of color to this background. It is a good thing as a rule to use plants that do not grow too high since it provides more scope for different arrangements in the restricted space available. Certain types of arrangement will even, by creating a feeling of perspective, make a balcony appear more spacious than it is.

Finally, an extremely useful kind of balcony-garden is the miniature herb garden. Perennial herbs such as Sage, Thyme, Sweet bay (Laurus nobilis), Chive (Allium), Tarragon (Artemisia drancunculus), and Savory (Satureja hortensis) will not only scent your balcony but will also season your cuisine.

1. Large pebbles and Fescue grasses provide a bed for Tulips, Lily, and Aubrietia

1. Here the adjacent vegetation brushes against the edge of the balcony, which constitutes a kind of floral transition
2. Clumps of Fescue grass enhance a Sage plant
3. Campanula and Periwinkle in the shade of a Cotoneaster
4. Nestling among huge pebbles, ferns, Stonecrop and Sage create a mountain landscape in miniature

1

2

3

4

1. A Climbing Persicary provides a visual link between this balcony and the adjacent wood, with a group of Crocus lending their colorful note
2. A Wisteria softens the rectangular stiffness of the woodwork here, offering a link between the house and the surrounding vegetation

1

1

2

3

3. A large concrete trough planted with a careful disarray of evergreen plants gives a see-through facade privacy and protection

1. The cantilevered plant troughs decorating this Japanese house project a facade of vegetation relieving the crude simplicity of the strips of unrendered concrete

1

XII. The Roof-Garden

The roof-garden—the ''dream'' of every city-dweller—offers, in spite of its generally restricted size and the technical constraints such as the need for complete water-tightness and the strength of the supporting structure, most of the features of a conventional garden planted in the soil. Consisting of one or more levels, it is relatively unaffected by questions of aspect, because it will receive light from all sides, unless a nearby building casts a shadow on it—in which case it will have to be designed accordingly. Here the function of the garden is decisive: either the garden will be designed purely to provide a pleasant view from the windows of the house or flat, or it will be made easily accessible and arranged in such a way as to accommodate a variety of family and social activities such as meals, games, and sun-bathing.

A roof-garden represents the logical extension of the building it serves; the architectural and horticultural aspects of its design need to be perfectly matched—not only outside but also when considered from inside the house. Indeed it may well be treated as having a foot in both camps, as it were, using various elements such as ponds, plant troughs, and paving to knit the two together.

The architectural aspect of the roof-garden is more important than the horticultural aspect. It will use all the components of the conventional garden such as pergolas, borders, flower beds, ponds, steps, rockeries, paving, and various walls and abutments. Given the limits imposed by floor strength, different types of paving will be the dominant element in the accessible roof-garden as representing the least extra weight in proportion to area. Textures will be carefully chosen in the light of the proposed function and the visual importance of the surface concerned, as well as of the plants furniture and accessories that will be placed there. Stairways, treated as lightly as possible, will link the different storeys and short flights of steps the

1. Around this sculptured bench an enclosing garden planted with perennials both marks a boundary and provides a visual link with the surrounding vegetation. Cobbles and a clump of rushes set off the concrete paving

intermediate, decorative levels. Pergolas may be used to join up sections of wall (lift shafts and chimneys), providing shady, intimate places for lounging or taking meals. A pond or a simple fountain will enliven any composition by its mere presence as well as by virtue of the aquatic plants in which they may be planted.

The horticultural aspect will bring a refining complement to the architectural arrangement. Careful thought must be given to color, perspective, and angle of view as well as to the question of relating to the surrounding vegetation. Weight considerations dictate the distribution of soil, most of which must be placed above load-bearing members (walls and uprights), and consequently the positioning of the major elements. Tubs of trees and shrubs for example are extremely heavy. In the case of the non-accessible roof-garden a layer of earth spread evenly to a depth of about 40 cm. can be planted with herbs, ornamental grasses, and a variety of low-growing or spreading plants according to season. Another good place for planting is the parapet, which can either be treated as a plant trough, made up from a wooden, aluminum, or plate-glass balustrade and planted with a mixture of various plants. Plant troughs can be treated as borders, as flower beds, or hedges.

1. A flight of terraces with their outlines broken with vegetation
2. Cotoneaster, rose, Petunia, and Aubrietia form a decorative protective hedge
3. Polygonum, Trumpet creeper, and climbing Geranium wash over the architecture like a breaking wave
4. A fine example of integration with the landscape

1

2

3

4

Aubrietia, rose, Fescue grass, Scabious (Scabiosa), Sage, Periwinkle, ferns, and various bulbs are often used in conjunction with evergreen shrubs. Pergolas can be decorated with climbers—Virgin's bower, Bignonia and Climbing Persicary—as can the various walls. A wall draped with the vine Ampelopsis, for example, will take on a quite different character.

Many other elements can contribute to the composition of a roof-garden including works of art, sculptures, fountains, arrangements of large and small pebbles, benches, tables, and so on. Lighting is an important factor as regards both beauty and habitability. The light sources can be concealed in the vegetation with perhaps a spot light here and there highlighting particular plants, or they can be bracket lamps on the walls or lamp standards to provide a diffuse light. The important point to be made is that they will reinforce the character of the garden, whether it be romantic, cosy, or grandiose.

That character, as expressed by the interplay of the constructed and cultivated elements, can also be made to change with the seasons; a different selection of annuals will, without altering the overall context, enliven in a natural way what is by definition an artificial arrangement. For surely in an entirely man-made roof-garden perched on top of what may be a very tall building, bathed in the pure air and the bright light high above the gloom and pollution of the city streets, it is the natural quality that is going to be most appreciated.

1. 2. Each terrace has its own decorative or functional character—depending on which level of the house it serves. The use of the same tiling lends unity to this composition

1

2

1. Nature is symbolized by a single tree in these bare and austere surroundings
2. An abstract composition of Fescue grasses and concrete
3. Gravel, Fescue grasses and unrendered concrete, relieved by a border of perennials

1

2

1. A large rose and a carpet of spreading perennials create a landscape in miniature
2. A Juniper hedge shields the accessible section of this terrace. The non-accessible section has been planted with a selection of low-growing and spreading perennials

1

2

XIII. A Roof-Garden in Paris

We felt we must give this Paris roof-garden a chapter of its own because since it combines all of the components of a traditional garden—paving, stairways, pergolas, a pond, borders, and flower beds—and because horticulturally, being designed as a piece of decoration rather than as a garden, it forms an exceptionally rich composition. It occupies a series of three terraces joined by straight or winding stairways, with each terrace having a separate function. The lowest of the three is fairly wide and communicates with the living room, which opens onto a paved area of Comblanchien limestone. A suite of garden furniture makes this a place for social life and

1. Arborvitae and Cypress are highlighted by Hydrangea, Rhododendron, and various evergreen shrubs (May)
2. The Quince in fruit catches the light against the dark green uprights of the Cypress hedge (October)
3. A flowering Orange and a Weeping Birch dance a pas de deux over a floor of annuals and spreaders (May)
4. At the foot of the flowering cherry veiling the stairway, Chrysanthemum and African Marigold decorate the border (October)
5. Multi-colored Petunias brighten the pond, which is planted with Iris, Arum, and Water-lily (May)
6. The richness of the autumn coloring is heightened by that of the Chrysanthemums (October)

7. The main terrace, punctuated by an Orange in a tub, an Araucaria, and a Dracaena, is bordered with Petunia, Begonia, Wallflower, and Impatiens (May)
8. In autumn the Pansies make their appearance. The bulbs are planted and will come up in late winter and early spring (October)
9. An Apple tree umbrella, a stone bench, and roses—the perfect lovers' corner (May)
10. Fruit has taken the place of leaves on this weeping Apple tree set in a sea of annuals around a Knee pine (October)

7

8   9   10

relaxation all summer long. An intimate pergola, complete with a swing, is tucked away round a corner. Decorating the central part is a pond planted with Iris, Arum, and Water-lily and enlivened by a small jet of water. The middle, smaller terrace offers a little nook—a stone bench under an Apple tree umbrella—that commands a most attractive view. There is room overlooking this terrace too, the terrace itself forming a canopy above the living room terrace. The top terrace, the largest of the three, is fitted out for golf and basketball training. A Cypress and an Holm oak (Quercus ilex) mark the corners—unusual silhouettes in the Paris sky.

There is a profusion of plants, and they are arranged in such a way as to have something flowering all the time. The flower beds are recomposed and entirely renewed every season.

In autumn it is the Chrysanthemums and the Honeysuckle that are in bloom. The Hawthorn berries are bright red. The plants that will spend the winter in flower are just coming out—Polyanthus in every color, yellow Jasmin, Pansies (Viola). When winter is over, Crocus, Hyacinth, Daffodil, Camellia, and Jonquil (Narcissus jonquilla) will herald the spring, which when full will be the heyday of a host of shrubs and flowers: Judas tree (Cercis siliquas-

trum), Forsythia, Mimosa (Acacia floribunda), Quince (Cydonia), Broom (Genista or Cytisus), Orange, Laburnum, Tulip, Alpine Forget-me-not, and Shepherd's purse (Capsella bursa-pastoris). Summer is the season of Cherry laurel (Prunus laurocerasus), Lilac (Syringa), Magnolia, Hydrangea, Geranium (Pelargonium), Petunia, Sage, Wallflower (Cheiranthus), Begonia, Ageratum, Gardenia, and many more.

The roses flower all the year round. Scented plants dotted about on all levels perfume the entire garden, and a little kitchen garden provides Strawberries (Fragaria) and aromatic herbs: Chives, Thyme, Rosemary, and Parsley (Petroselinum crispum).

1. The bedroom is progressively shut off from view
2. 3. The spiral staircase emerges from a profusion of vegetation, to which it stands in elegant contrast

1

2

3

1

2

3

1. Looking towards the living room
2. The bedroom with its private garden
3. The walk on the middle terrace

140

Plans

The letters appearing on the architectural plans are explained in the key on p. 162 (flap). The numbers on the horticultural plans refer to the index of plants on pp. 155 ff.

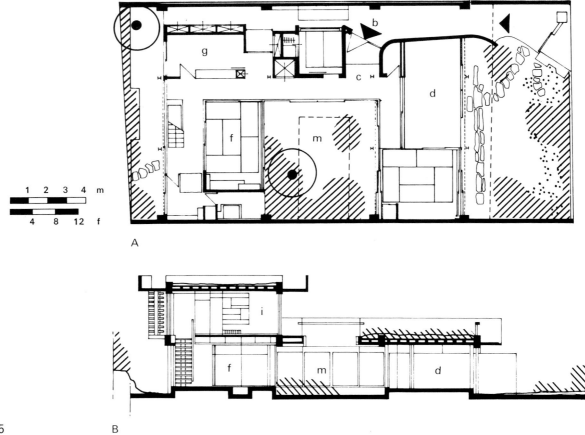

A

B

I Architect:
Junzo Sakakura, Tokyo
See illustrations on pp. 80/1, 85/5

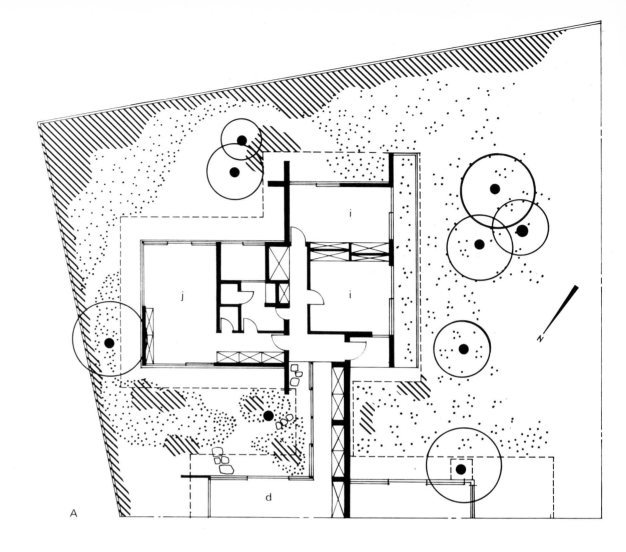

II Architect:
Junzo Sakakura, Tokyo
See illustrations on pp. 85/3-4, 86/1

A

1 2 3 4 m

4 8 12 f

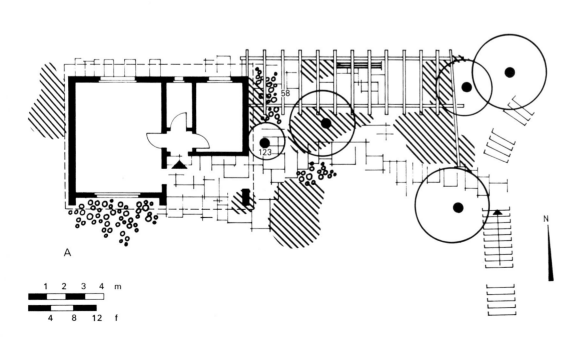

A

1 2 3 4 m

4 8 12 f

III Architect:
Reinhold Willumeit, Darmstadt-Eberstadt
See illustrations on pp. 44/2, 76/1

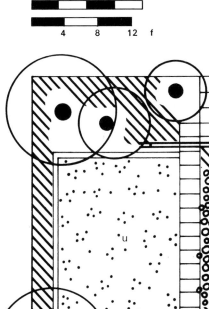

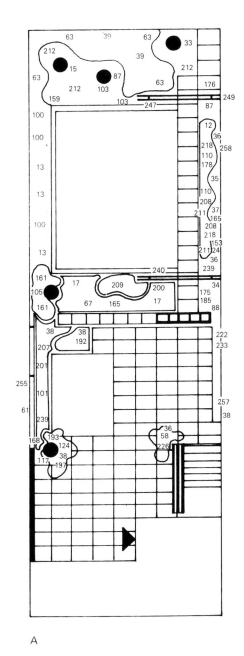

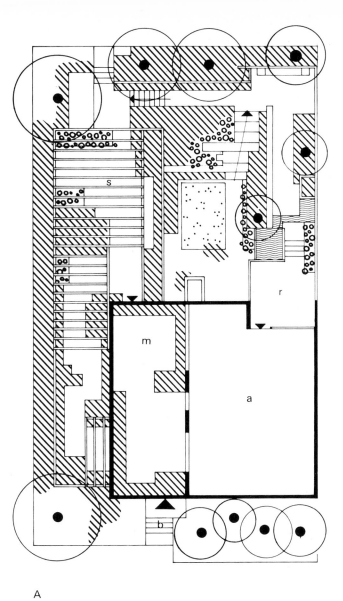

A

A

A

VI   Architects:
Hans Luz, Rudi Volz, Stuttgart
See illustrations on pp. 33/1, 37/6, 104/1

IV   Architects:
Wolfgang Mueller, Gregor Schmitz, Willich
V   Cf. IV
See illustrations on pp. 30/2, 46/2, 60/1

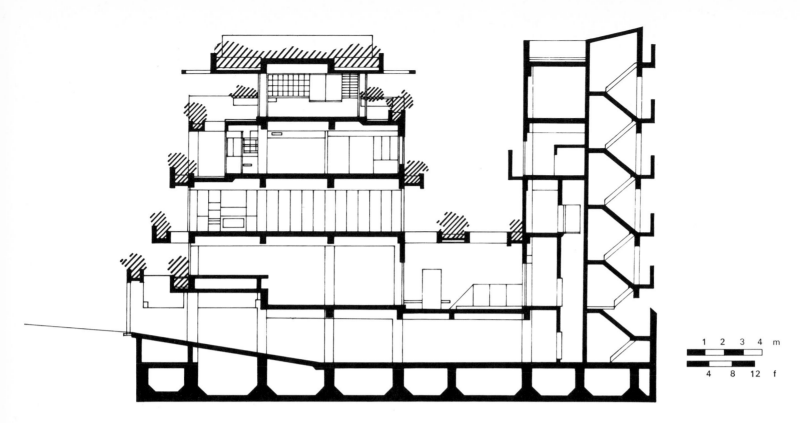

B

VII   Architect:
Junzo Sakakura, Tokyo
See illustration on p. 124/1

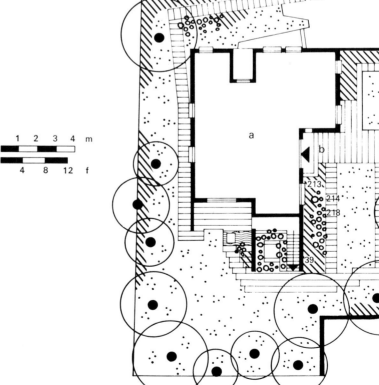

VIII   Architect:
G. Kühn, Köln
See illustrations on pp. 48/1, 66/1   A

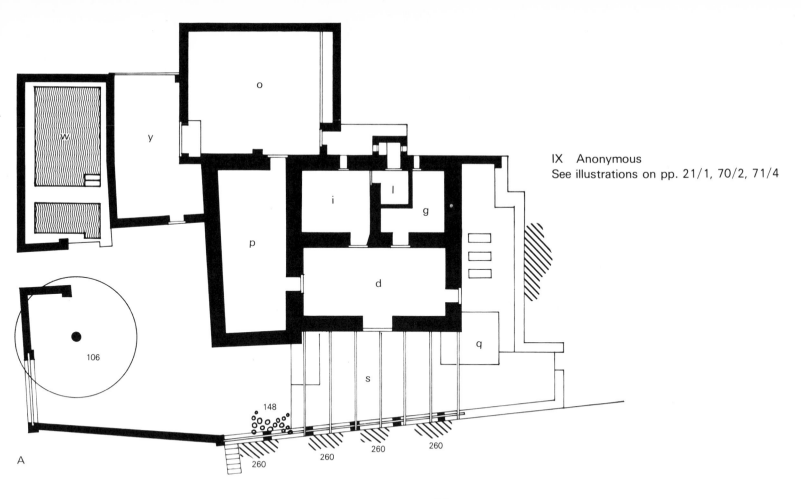

IX Anonymous
See illustrations on pp. 21/1, 70/2, 71/4

1 2 3 4 m

4 8 12 f

X Architect:
Gordon Patterson, Aston-Hertfordshire
See illustrations on p. 25/1-3

1 2 3 4 m

4 8 12 f

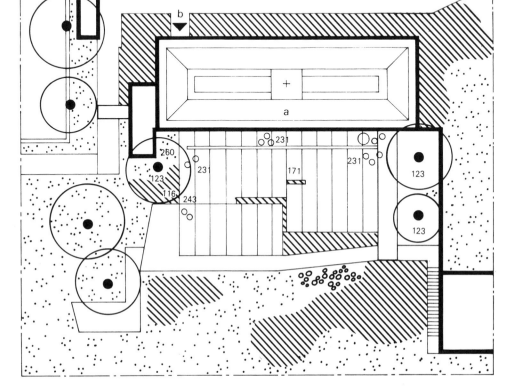

A

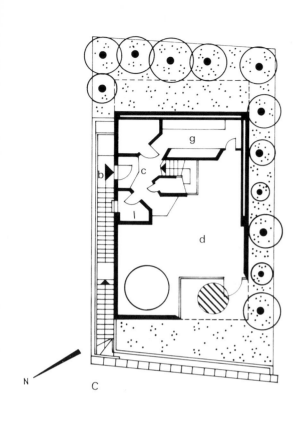

C

XI   Architects:
Mayumi Myawaki & Associates, Tokyo
See illustrations on p. 84/1-2

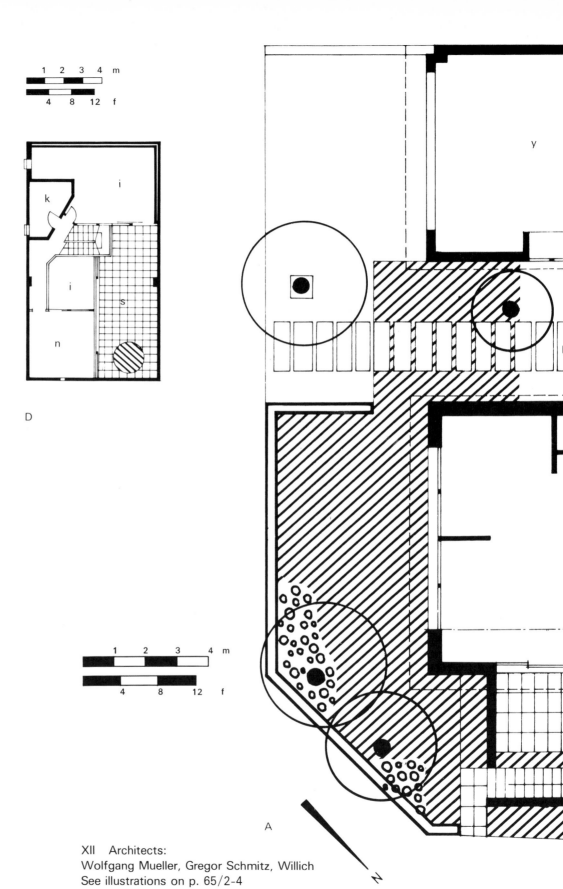

D

XII   Architects:
Wolfgang Mueller, Gregor Schmitz, Willich
See illustrations on p. 65/2-4

A

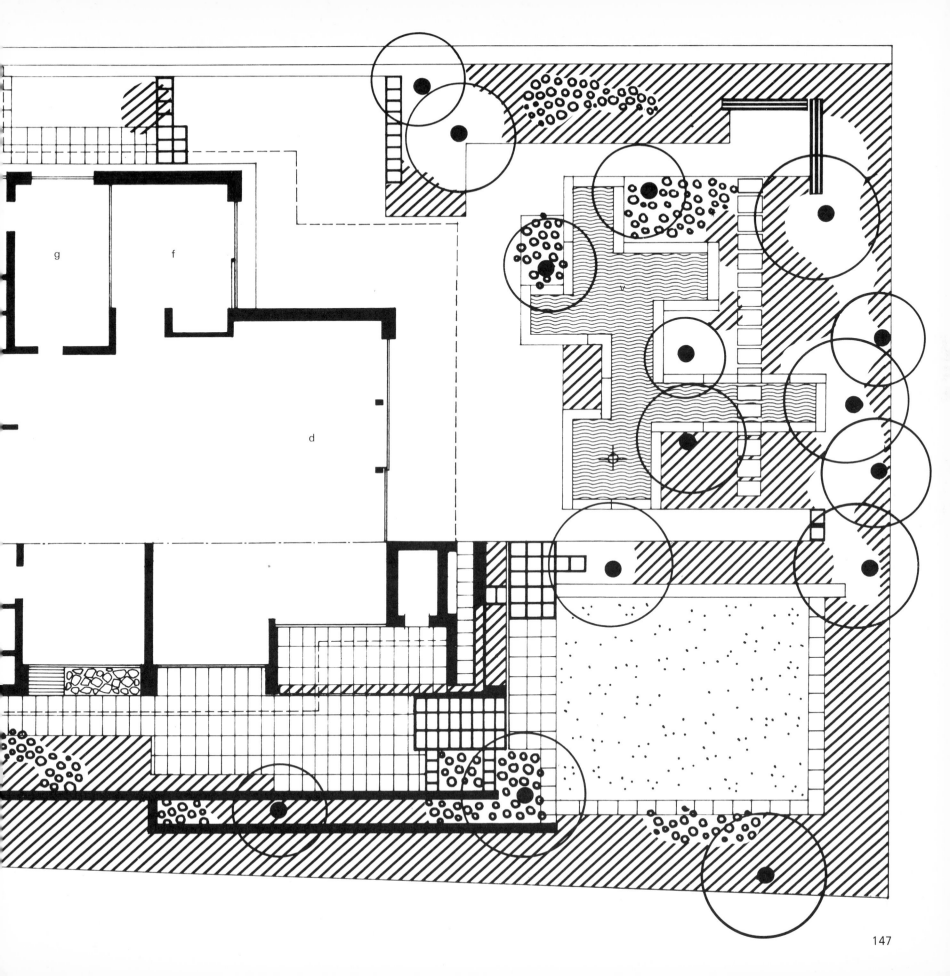

g

f

d

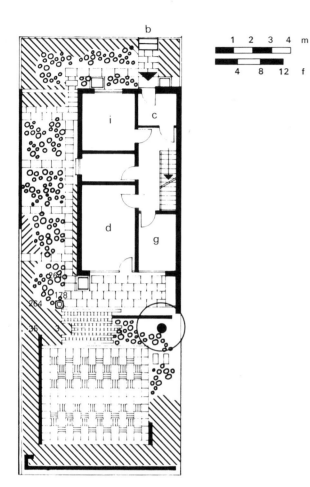

A

XIII   Architect:
Peter Wirth, Echterdingen
See illustrations on pp. 29/4-5, 44/1, 63/5,
101/1-2

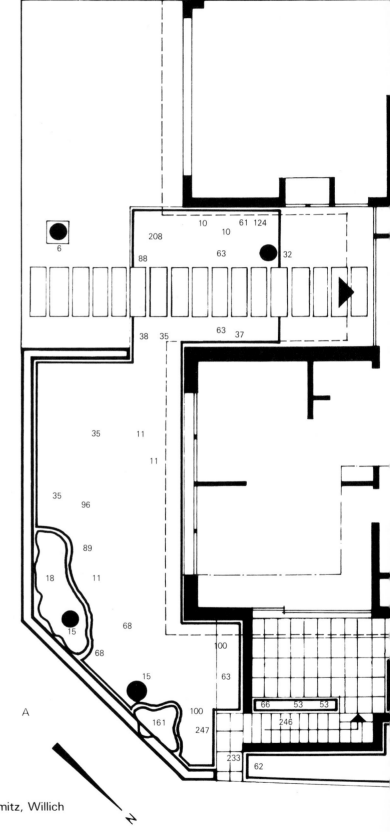

A

XIV   Architects:
Wolfgang Mueller, Gregor Schmitz, Willich
See illustrations on p. 65/2-4

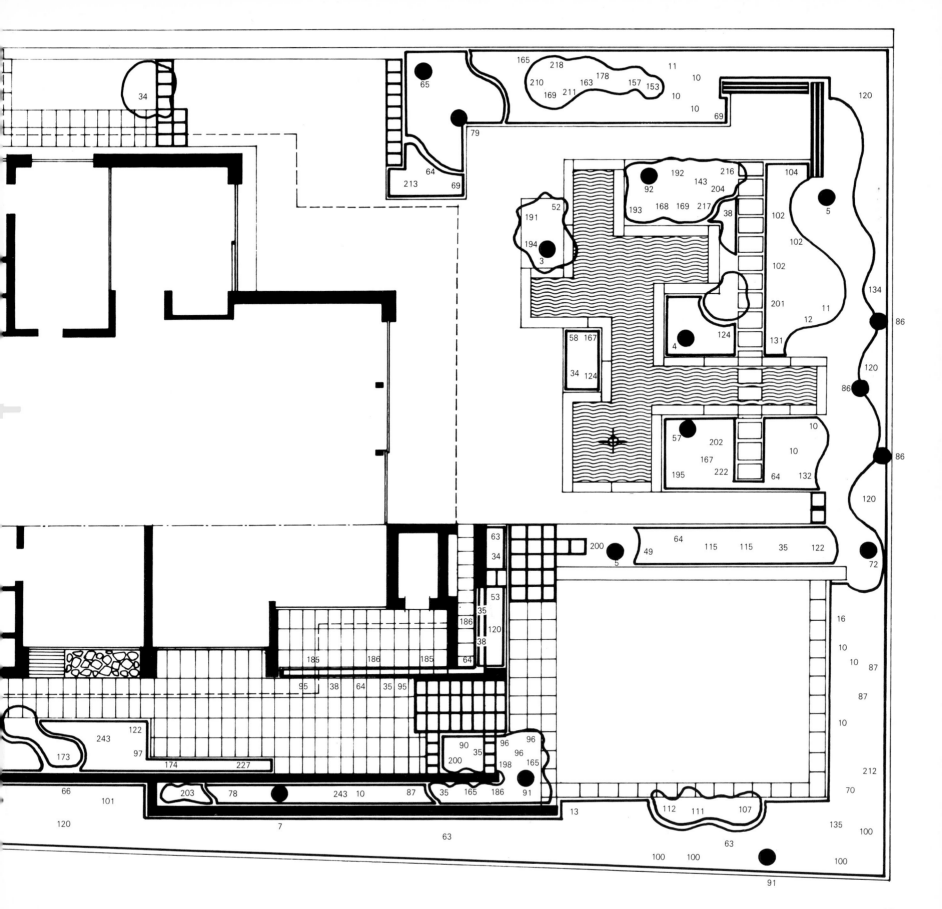

149

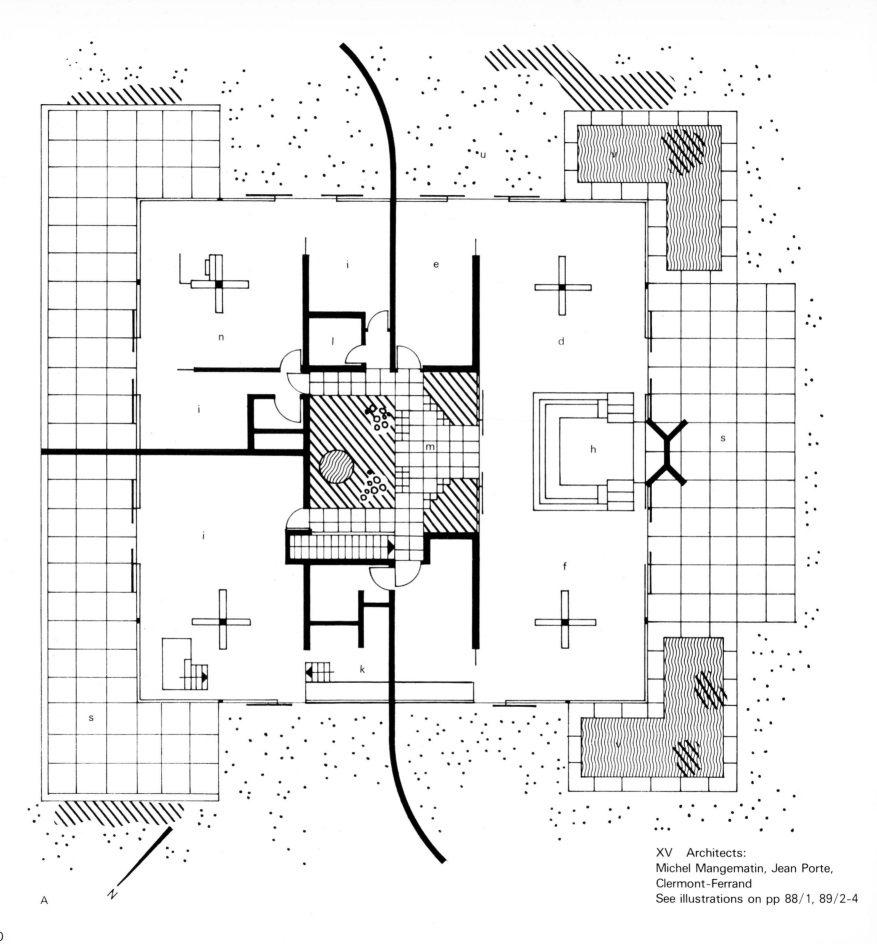

A

N

XV Architects:
Michel Mangematin, Jean Porte,
Clermont-Ferrand
See illustrations on pp 88/1, 89/2-4

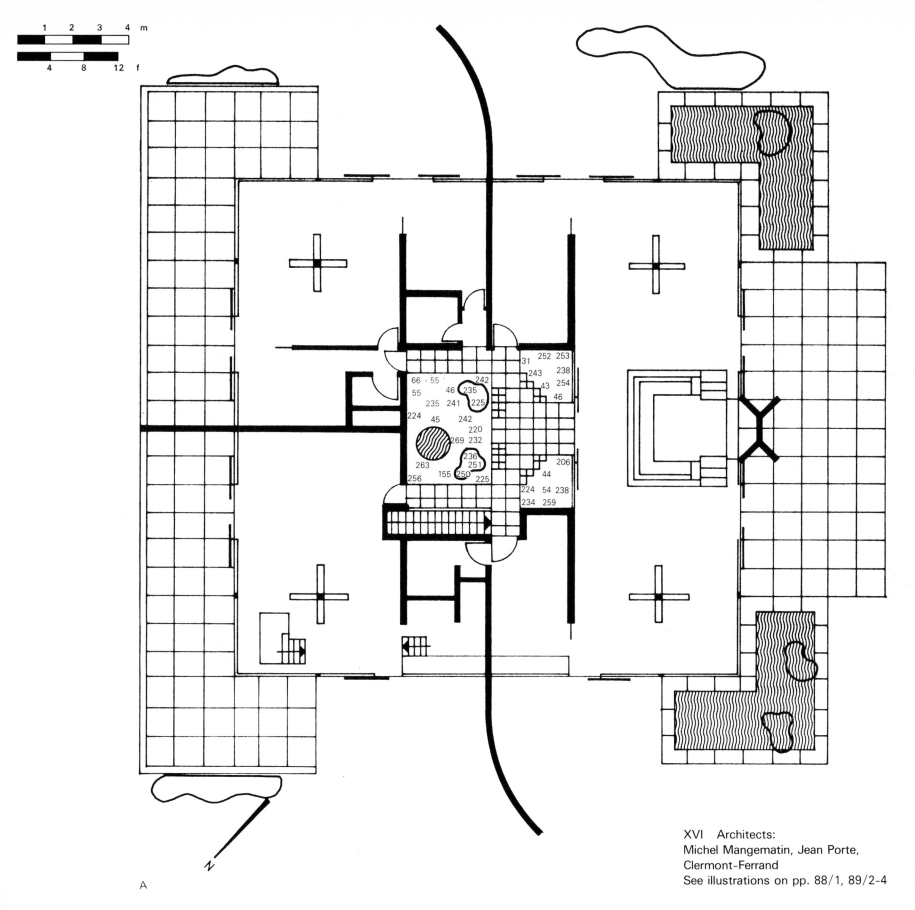

1 2 3 4 m

4 8 12 f

252 253
31 238
243
66 · 55 242 43 254
55 46 235 46
235 241 225
224 45 242
220
269 232
263 236
251 206
256 155 250 225 44
224 54 238
234 259

N

A

XVI   Architects:
Michel Mangematin, Jean Porte,
Clermont-Ferrand
See illustrations on pp. 88/1, 89/2-4

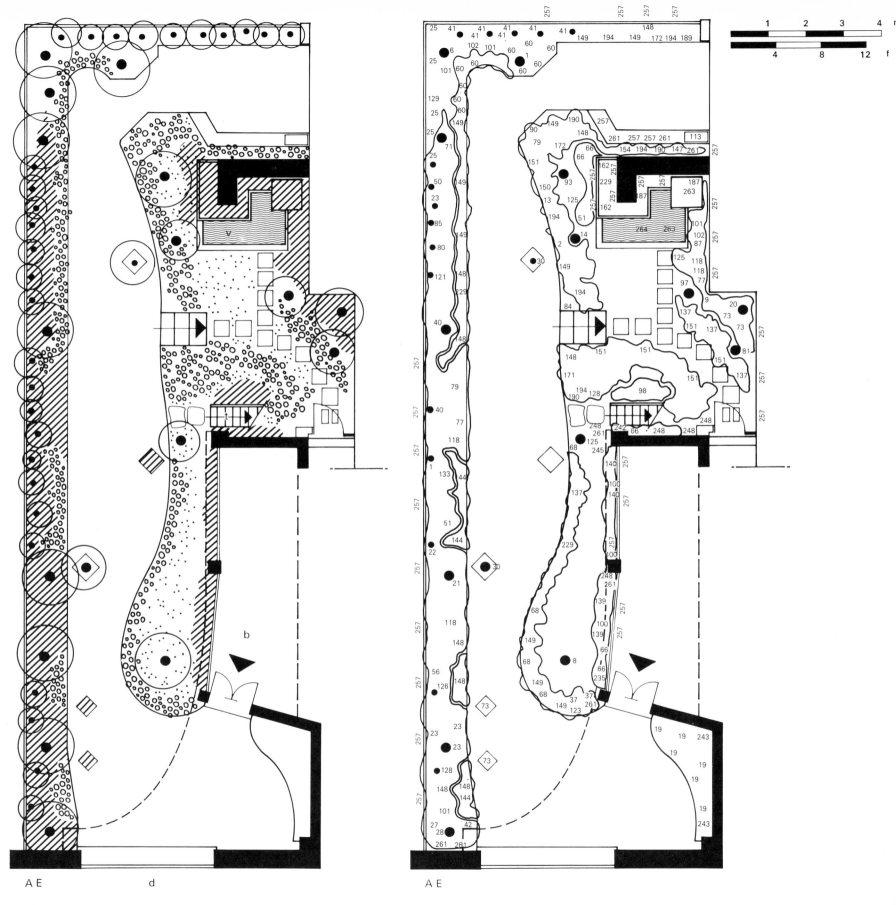

XVII Architect:
R. Sockeel, Paris
XVIII Cf. XVII
See illustrations on pp. 136, 137, 139 140

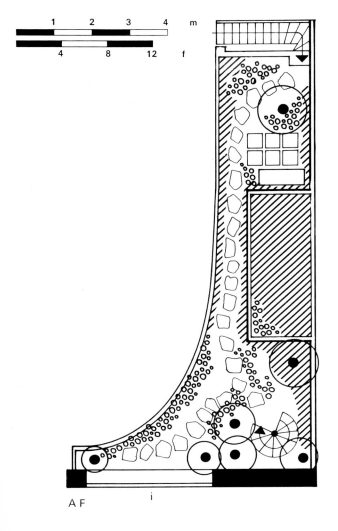

A F

XIX Architect:
R. Sockeel, Paris
XX Cf. XIX
See illustrations on pp. 136, 137, 139,140

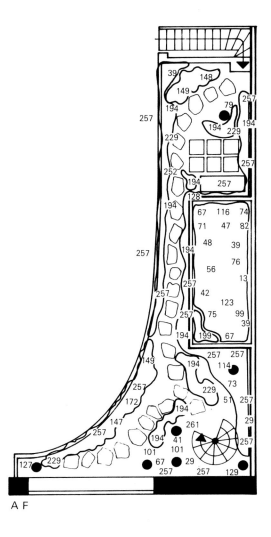

A F

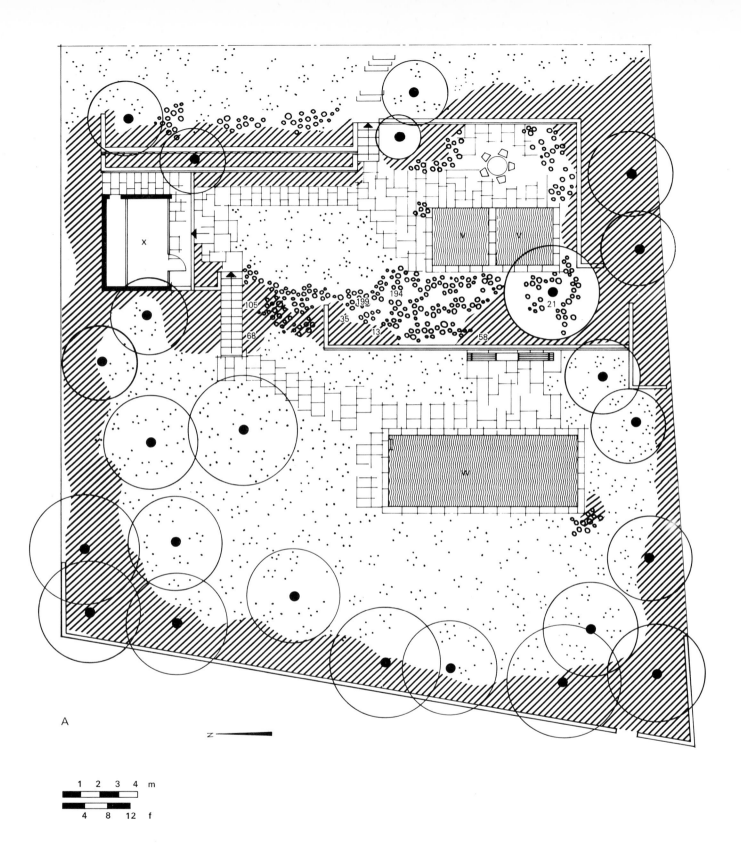

A

| 1 | 2 | 3 | 4 | m |

| 4 | 8 | 12 | f |

XXI   Architect:
Reinhold Willumeit, Darmstadt-Eberstadt
See illustrations on pp. 47/3, 59/3, 76/2, 101/4

Index of plants

Listed here are all the plants that appear either on the plans or in the main illustrations. The references are in the last column of the table. The Roman numerals refer to plans (pp. 141-154) and the page-numbers to the illustrations.

The Latin name is followed by the most widely-used common name or names, where such exist (often in English the Latin name has been adopted as the "common" name). In some cases the common name is given for the genus only, the species and varieties being referred to by their Latin names.

Trees and shrubs

1	Acacia floribunda	Mimosa	XVIII
2	Acer palmatum var. dissectum		XVIII
3	Acer japonicum c.v. aconitifolium	Japanese maple	XIII, XIV; p. 26/2
4	Acer palmatum		XIV; p. 23/1
5	Acer saccharinum	Montpelier maple, white maple	XIV
6	Acer platanoides	Norway maple	XIV, XVIII
7	Aesculus hyppocastanum	Horse Chestnut	XIV
8	Araucaria	Monkey puzzle tree	p. 137/8
9	Azalea amoena (Rhododendron amoenum)		XVIII
10	Azalea japonica	Japanese azalea	XIV
11	Azalea mollis (Rhododendron molle)	Soft azalea	XIV
12	Azalea pontica (Rhododendron lutea)		V, XIV
13	Berberis thunbergii c.v. "Atropurpurea"	Barberry	V, XIV, XVIII, XX, XXI
14	Betula pendula	Weeping birch	XVIII
15	Betula verrucosa	Silver or white birch	V, XIV
16	Buddleja davidii	Butterfly bush	XIV
17	Calluna vulgaris c.v. "Alportii"	Ling, Heather	V
18	Calluna vulgaris c.v. "J.H. Hamilton"		XIV
19	Camellia japonica	Japanese camellia	XVIII
20	Carpinus betulus	Common hornbeam	XVIII
21	Cedrus atlantica var. glauca	Blue Atlas cedar	XVIII, XXI
22	Cercis siliquastrum	Judas tree	XVIII
23	Chaenomeles lagenaria	Japonica, Japanese quince	XVIII
24	Chaenomeles lagenaria c.v. "Crimson Gold"		V
25	Chamaecyparis lawsoniana		XVIII
26	Chamaecyparis lawsoniana c.v. "Allumii"		p. 140/1
27	Chamaecyparis lawsoniana c.v. "Columnaris Glauca"	False or Lawson's cypress	XVIII
28	Chamaecyparis lawsoniana c.v. "Elwoodii"		XVIII
29	Chamaecyparis lawsoniana c.v. "Fletcheri Nana"		XX
30	Citrus sinensis	Sweet orange	XVIII
31	Codiaeum variegatum c.v. "Pictum"	Croton, variegated laurel	XVI
32	Cornus florida	American dogwood	XIV
33	Cornus mas	European dogwood or Cornelian cherry	V
34	Cotoneaster adressus		V, XIV
35	Cotoneaster dammeri var. radicans		V, XIII, XIV, XXI
36	Cotoneaster dammeri var. radicans c.v. "Skogsholmen"	Cotoneasters	V
37	Cotoneaster horizontalis		V, XIV, XVIII
38	Cotoneaster microphylla		V, XIV
39	Cotoneaster salicifolius c.v. "Parkteppich"		V, VIII, XX
40	Cupressus arizonica c.v. "Conica"	Rough barked Arizona cypress	XVIII

41	Cupressus macrocarpa	Monterey cypress	XVIII, XX
42	Cytisus scoparius	Colliers Broom	XVIII, XX
43	Dieffenbachia amoena	Dumb cane	XVI
44	Dracaena fragrans	⎫	XVI
45	Dracaena marginata	⎬ Dragon trees	XVI
46	Dracaena sanderiana	⎭	XVI
47	Eleagnus angustifolia	Oleaster, Russian olive, Trebizond date	XX
48	Eleagnus pungens var. maculata		XX
49	Enkianthus campanulatus		XIV
50	Eucalyptus	Gum tree	XVIII
51	Euonymus aurea var. marginatus	⎫	XVIII, XX
52	Euonymus fortunei varo colorata	⎬ Spindle-trees	XIV
53	Euonymus fortunei var. vegetus	⎭	XIV
54	Ficus elastica	Rubber plant	XVI
55	Ficus lyrata	Garden fig	XVI; p. 95/1
56	Forsythia europaeus		XVIII, XX
57	Hamamelis mollis	Witch hazel	XIV
58	Helianthemum	Rock rose	III, V, XIV, XXI
59	Hibiscus rosa-sinensis	Rose of China, Hibiscus	p. 27/3, 38/1
60	Hydrangea macrophylla c.v. hortensia	Lace Cups, mop Head hydrangea	XVIII; p. 92/1
61	Hydrangea petiolaris	Climbing hydrangea	V, XIV
62	Hydrangea aspera subsp. sargentiana		XIV
63	Hypericum calycinum	St John's wort	V, XIV
64	Hypericum patulum c.v. "Hidcote"		XIV
65	Ilex aquifolium	Holly	XIV
66	Jasminum nudiflorum	Winter Jasmine	XIV, XVIII
67	Juniperus media var. aurea	⎫	V, XX
68	Juniperus media var. pfitzeriana	⎬ Junipers	XIV, XVIII, XXI
69	Juniperus repanda	⎭	XIV
70	Laburnum		XIV
71	Lagerstroemia indica	Crape-myrtle	XVIII, XX
72	Larix decidua	Larch	XIV
73	Laurus nobilis	Sweet bay	XVIII, XX
74	Ligustrum ovalifolium var. variegatum	Variegated privet	XX
75	Ligustrum ovalifolium var. aureum	Golden privet	XX
76	Ligustrum ovalifolium	Japanese privet	XX
77	Magnolia grandifolia	Bull bay	XVIII
78	Mahonia aquifolium	Oregon grape	XIV
79	Malus	Apple	XIV, XVIII, XX
80	Mespilus germanica	Medlar	XVIII
81	Olea europea	Olive	XVIII
82	Philadelphus	Mock orange	XX
83	Phoenix	Date palm	p. 79/1
84	Picea glauca c.v. "Conica"	White spruce	XVIII
85	Picea kosteriana	Blue spruce	XVIII
86	Picea amorika	Servian spruce	XIV
87	Pieris japonica	Japanese lavender heath	V, XIV, XVIII
88	Pinus mugo	Dwarf mountain pine	V, XIV
89	Pinus mugo var. pumilio	⎫	XIV
90	Pinus mugo var. mugo	⎬ Swiss mountain pines	XIV, XVIII; p. 46/2
91	Pinus nigra	Black pine, Austrian pine	XIV
92	Pinus parviflora	Japanese white pine	XIV
93	Pinus strobus	White pine	XVIII
94	Euphorbia pulcherrima	Poinsettia	p. 27/3
95	Potentilla arbuscula	⎫ Cinquefoils	XIV
96	Potentilla fruticosa	⎭	XIV
97	Prunus pissardi	Wax cherry	XIV, XVIII
98	Prunus serrulata c.v. "New Red"	Japanese flowering cherry	XVIII
99	Prunus triloba	Chinese almond	XX
100	Pyracantha coccinea	Firethorn	V, XIV, XVIII

101	Rhododendron praecox		V, XIV, XVIII, XX
102	Rhododendron repens	Rhododendrons	XIV, XVIII
103	Rhododendron repens c.v. "Scarlet Wonder"		V
104	Rhododendron williamsianum		XIV; p. 28/1
105	Rhus coridria	Sumach	V, XXI
106	Robinia pseudacacia	False acacia	IX· p. 21/1
107	Rosa floribunda c.v. "Lili Marleen"		XIV
108	Rosa c.v. golden howers		
109	Rosa c.v. Heidelberg		
110	Rosa c.v. K. Duvigneau	Roses	V
111	Rosa polyantha c.v. "All Gold"		XIV
112	Rosa polyantha c.v. "Gloria Dei"		XIV
113	Rosmarinus officinalis	Rosemary	XVIII
114	Schinus molle	Pepper tree	XX
115	Sinoarundinaria	Bamboo	XIV; p. 35/2, 43/1, 55/1
116	Skimmia japonica		X, XX
117	Sorbus aucuparia	Rowan tree	V
118	Spartium junceum	Spanish broom	XVIII
119	Spiraea bullata		p. 29/3
120	Symphoricarpus albus	Snowberry	XIV
121	Syringa vulgaris	Lilac	XVIII
122	Taxus aprather		XIV
123	Taxus baccata	Yews	II, X, XVIII, XX
124	Taxus baccata var. repandens		V, XIV
125	Taxus baccata var. aurea	Golden Yew	XVIII
126	Taxus baccata var. fastigiata	Irish Yew	XVIII
127	Thuya occidentalis	White cedar, America Arborvitae	XX
128	Thuya orientalis	Oriental Arborvitae, Chinese Arborvitae	XVIII
129	Thuya plicata var. atrovirens	Giant Arborvitae, Red Cedar	XVIII, XX
130	Ulex europaeus	Broom or Furze	p. 127/1
131	Viburnum carlesii		XIV
132	Viburnum rhytidophyllum		XIV
133	Viburnum tinus	Laurustinus	XVIII
134	Viburnum tomentosum c.v. "Mariesii"		XIV
135	Weigela floribunda		XIV
136	Yucca		p. 109/1

Annuals and biennials

137	Ageratum		XVIII
138	Althaea rosea	Hollyhock	p. 76/1
139	Antirrhinum	Wallflower	XVIII
140	Calceolaria	Lady's slipper	XVIII
141	Digitalis	Foxglove	p. 53/1
142	Gypsophila paniculata	Baby's breath	p. 44/2
143	Helianthus annuus	Sunflower	XIV
144	Impatiens		XVIII
145	Ipomoea	Morning glory	p. 99/2
146	Myosotis alpestris	Alpine forget-me-not	p. 30/1
147	Pelargonium hortorum	Geranium	XVIII, XX
148	Pelargonium peltatum	Ivy-leaved geranium	IX, XVIII, XX; p. 25/1
149	Petunia		XVIII, XX
150	Salvia horminum	Sage	XVIII
151	Tagetes patula	French marigold	XVIII
152	Verbena officinalis	Vervain	p.29/3

Perennials and rockery plants

153	Achillea filipéndula	Milfoil	V, XIV
154	Alyssum		XVIII; p. 111/1
155	Anthurium andreanum		XVI
156	Aquilegia vulgaris	Columbine	p. 43/1
157	Arabis procurrens	Rock cress	XIV
158	Arum creticum		p. 89/3, 136/5
159	Aruncus sylvester (Spiraea aruncus)	Goat's beard	V
160	Aster	Starwort	29/7
161	Aster dumosus		V, XIV
162	Astilbe cattleya		XVIII
163	Aubrietia		XIV
164	Aubrietia deltoida c.v. "Neuling"		p. 51/1
165	Avena candida	Oats	V, XIV
166	Begonia socotrana	Christmas begonia	p. 25/1
167	Bergenia cordifolia	Heart-leaf saxifrage	XIV
168	Caltha palustris	Marsh Marigold	V, XIV
169	Campanula carpatica	Bell flower	XIV; p. 44/2
170	Canna	Sennapod	p. 63/2
171	Cerastium	Chickweed	X, XVIII
172	Chrysanthemum		XVIII, XX
173	Cimicifuga racemosa	Bugbane	XIV
174	Convallaria majalis	Lily-of-the-valley	XIV; p. 103/1
175	Coreopsis verticillata	Tickseed	V
176	Cortaderria	Pampas grass	V
177	Cyperus papyrus	Papyrus	p. 89/2, 136/5
178	Delphinium	Larkspurs	V, XIII, XIV
179	Delphinium alternifolia		p. 29/3, 43/1, 44/2
180	Dianthus	Pink	p. 45/3
181	Doronicum cordatum	Leopard's bane	p. 30/1
182	Epiphyllum	Leaf cactus	p. 96/1
183	Erica carnea	Mediterranean heather	p. 59/2
184	Euphorbia	Spurge	p. 92/1
185	Festuca glauca	Fescue grasses	V, XIV; p. 23/2, 38/1
186	Festuca scoparia		p. 65/2
187	Fuchsia magellanica c.v. "Riccartonii"		XVIII
188	Funkia fortunei (Hosta)	Plantain lily, day-lily	p. 33/1, 38/2
189	Gardenia		XVIII
190	Gazania		XVIII
191	Hemerocallis	Day-lily	XIV
192	Hemerocallis citrina	Yellow day-lily	V, XIV
193	Hosta (Funkia)	Plantain lily, day-lily	V, XIV
194	Iberis sempervirens	Candytuft	XIV, XVIII, XX, XXI; p. 44/2
195	Iris laevigata	Japanese Iris	XIV; p. 43/1
196	Iris sibirica var. alba	Siberian Iris	p. 65/2
197	Iris sibirica c.v. "Perrys Blue"		V, XX
198	Kniphofia	Red-hot poker	XIV
199	Lavandula	Lavender	XX, XXI
200	Liatris spicata	Blazing star	V, XIV
201	Ligularia x. hessei		V, XIV
202	Senecis przewalskii		XIV
203	Lysimachia punctata	Loosestrife	XIV
204	Lythrum salicaria	Purple loosestrife	XIV
205	Macleaya cordata	Plume poppy	p. 65/4
206	Maranta leuconeura var. massangeana	Prayer plant	XVI
207	Miscanthus sinensis var. gigantis	Eulalias	V
208	Miscanthus sinensis var. gracilis		V, XIV
209	Miscanthus sinensis var. zebinus		V
210	Oenothera glauca	Evening primroses	XIV
211	Oenothera missouriensis		V, XIV

212	Pachysandra terminalis		V, XIV
213	Pennisetum		VIII, XIV; p. 48/1
214	Phlox		VIII; p. 48/1
215	Potentilla	Cinquefoil	p. 63/3
216	Rodgersia aesculifolia		XIV
217	Rodgersia tabularis		XIV
218	Rudbeckia speciosa c.v. "Sullivantii Goldsturm"	Coneflower	V, VIII, XIV; p. 29/5, 38/1
219	Salvia	Sage	p. 118/2, 119/4
220	Sansevieria trifasciata	Snake plant, Leopard lily, bowstring hemp	XVI
221	Saxifraga	Saxifrage	
222	Sedum spurium c.v. "Schorbusser Blut"	Stonecrop	V, XIV
223	Sempervivum	Houseleek	p. 119/4
224	Tradescantia virginiana var. albiflora	Spiderworts	XVI, p. 89/2
225	Tradescantia virginiana var. fluminensis		XVI
226	Veronica latifolia	Broad-leaved Speedwell	V
227	Vinca minor	Lesser periwinkle	XIV; p. 118/3

Bulbed plants

228	Allium scholnoprasum	Chives	p. 96/1
229	Begonia tuberhybrida var. multiflora		XVIII, XX
230	Crocus		p. 120/1
231	Tulipa	Tulip	X; p. 25/2-3

Climbers

232	Allamanda cathartica c.v. "Grandiflora"		XVI
233	Aristolochia durior	Birthwort	V, XIV
234	Asparagus plumosus	Asparagus fern	XVI
235	Bougainvillaea		XVI, XVIII; p. 71/1
236	Brassocattleya cliftonii c.v. "Magnifica"	Orchid	XVI
237	Campsis	Trumpet creeper	p. 129/3
238	Cissus antarctica	Kangaroo-vine	XVI
239	Clematis virginiana c.v. "Jackmanii"	Virgin's bower	V
240	Clematis virginiana c.v. "Nelly Moser"		V
241	Ficus repens	Creeping fig	XVI
242	Hedera canariensis	Canary ivy	XVI, XVIII
243	Hedera helix	Ivy	X, XIV, XVI, XVIII
244	Hedera helix c.v. hibernica	Irish ivy	
245	Lonicera japonica var. chinensis	Honeysuckles	XVIII
246	Lonicera fuchsioides		XIV
247	Lonicera henryi		V, XIV
248	Lonicera japonica		XVIII
249	Lonicera x. tellmanniana		V
250	Odontoglossum x. c.v. kopan "Lyoth Aura"	Orchid	XVI
251	Passiflora caerulea	Passion-flower	XVI
252	Philodendron hastatum		XVI, XX
253	Philodendron laciniatum		XVI
254	Monstera deliciosa	Cheese plant	XVI
255	Polygonum aubertii	Climbing Persicary	V
256	Pothos aureus		XVI
257	Rosa	Roses	V, XVIII, XX
258	Rosa c.v. "Don Juan"		V
259	Stephanotis floribunda		XVI
260	Vitis vinifera	Vine, Grape-vine	IX, X; p. 30/5